PRAISE FOR BORN OF BETRAYAL

"Betrayal is one of the most common ways in which women lose their power and feel very isolated from others. Ali courageously shares what she learned during a tough betrayal and how she transformed her life into one of success, love and happiness. She's raw and real. This book will bring you to tears then lead you to hope and transformation. I highly recommend this book to anyone who has or is suffering from a betrayal."

> — Rachael Jayne Groover, Creator of Art of Feminine Presence and best-selling author of *Powerful and Feminine* and *Divine Breadcrumbs*.

"Many people experience betrayal in one form or another. The severity depends on the situation, the people involved, and our own wellness at the time. Ali guides us in understanding that we don't need to forgive others to heal ourselves. The story focuses on the importance of knowing yourself, loving yourself, and forgiving yourself. After reading this book, I was left with hope and a deep knowing that I am not alone. I highly recommend this book and I encourage you to purchase extra copies because you will want to share it with everyone you know!"

> — Jewels Muller, Founder, Chicks Connect Mastermind Support Network

"Have you ever felt confused and questioned who you are and your own decision-making abilities after experiencing betrayal? We all define betrayal differently and we respond to the sense of anger, grief, and loss in our own unique way. In using the metaphor of the transformation to a beautiful butterfly from the humble beginnings of a caterpillar, the author shares with us through her own insights how she leaned on her faith in Spirit and her strong self-resolve to bounce back from profound betrayal. Through the author's writing, we discover and take solace in knowing that we are not alone in our feelings. I highly recommend this book for anyone seeking real-life resources in healing the emotional wounds that keep us from thriving after loss and emotional abandonment."

— Michele Duncan King, Coach and Celebrant,
  Founder of Poppy + Veil

Born of
BETRAYAL

From Breakdown to Breakthrough

ALI DAVIDSON

Born of Betrayal: From Breakdown to Breakthrough

First Edition, November 2020

Published by Ali Davidson Coaching, LLC
Tualatin, OR

www.bornofbetrayal.com

Editorial services by Suzanne Reamy

Front cover artist: Urmi Boyd

ISBN 978-1-7356695-2-6 Paperback Edition
ISBN 978-1-7356695-0-2 Digitaal Edition
ISBN 978-1-7356695-1-9 Hardcover Edition
ISBN 978-1-7356695-3-3 Audiobook Edition

Library of Congress Control Number: 2020916290

Printed in the United States of America

DEDICATION

I dedicate this book to all the courageous women who are learning how to fly. Transformation is what is born of betrayal: your colors will be brilliant; your wings, strong—your destiny is waiting for you. Let your heart open wide to the gifts of your pain for this breakdown will lead you to the breakthrough your soul has been longing for. And sister, you are not alone! Ever...

The caterpillar, born on a tree on which it
will live its entire existence,
will spend a lifetime eating and growing,
then eating and growing some more.
Until one day, having grown as much as it
was able, having shed as many shells as it
could, it is compelled from deep inside to
create a cocoon and entrap itself within.
The caterpillar has no idea that this
cocoon will be its death,
that within this soft threaded world it will
liquefy and be no more.
Within this soup are the imaginal cells
that lived dormant in the caterpillar
which will come together at this time and
give birth to a whole new creature,
one that no longer crawls along leaves,
but instead, has wings that will allow it to
discover whole new worlds. Once the
transmutation is complete, the butterfly
emerges, spreads its wings, and spends
her life fluttering from blossom to bloom,
and tree to leaf until she is ready
to give life to another caterpillar.
And the cycle continues.

Welcome to the Butterfly Quest

FROM THE AUTHOR

All transitions start with an ending of something, some big thing that happens which feels out of your control. Something that hurts, feels unsafe, sends you into the dark night of the soul. After we have suffered the ending and learned to accept it, we move into the time I call "the in-between," where we are no longer who we used to be, but are not yet who we will become. It is a time of soul searching, a time of chaos, of quiet reflection—sometimes lonely, sometimes frightening, but always revealing. And then one day, you wake up and something feels different. You have moved from the in-between into the time of beginnings. Our transformation is no less miraculous than that of the butterfly. It is a time of awakening to our soul, letting go of the life we once knew and stepping into something so drastically changed that we hardly recognize ourselves. For the first time in a long while, you feel hopeful. You begin to feel the stirrings of a new dream. Your passion for life has been restored in a new way, in a new life. And you are transformed.

From the very first moment my life came crashing

down around me almost six years ago, I knew Spirit was getting me ready to write my next book. I knew the life I'd known was dissolving and someday I'd understand why. All of us, at some point, suffer through challenges, and yet everywhere you look there is someone saying, "do this and all will be well." I have been a counselor and coach for almost 25 years. I've developed and facilitated many personal growth workshops. I've also written books with the intention of helping others. Giving the answers I have found worked, not only for me, but also for my clients. But this book was different because when I started writing it, I had yet to find the answers. I wasn't through the pain. I hadn't completely healed, and I didn't want to sound like a victim, a woman scorned, some ranting lunatic who just needed to give voice to the things that had happened.

When I started this book, my pain hit me in the gut each day. No matter how hard I tried to "soothe my inner child," "raise my vibration," "state positive affirmations," "meditate to clear my mind," "take a walk in nature," or "distract myself with friends and fun," I wasn't ready to say "thank you" to the experience that had caused such upheaval in my life.

I believe we are always getting direction on the path of our lives, little nudges saying "this way baby"—this way to the next evolutionary experience your soul has come to have. But when we don't listen, well…as the saying goes, shift happens. It has to happen. We are forced to change by what seems to be life circumstances, and we do in fact change directions, though we might go kicking and screaming. I know I did. For a while we feel lost, stranded at a dead end, abandoned not only by others, but also by ourselves. One might say that we've been given a wakeup call. We've been asleep in our own lives. And the waking is jolting, disorienting, and uncomfortable to say the least.

My wakeup call came when my life fell apart.

Eight months later, God sent his angels in many forms to give me a message. Yup, that's right. I have always believed that when things happen in threes, they are meant to be. It's God's way of saying, "Hey, listen up!"

The first message came when I was sitting in the middle of an auditorium filled with twenty-five hundred people. It was Louise Hay's "I Can Do It" conference… and it was my birthday, the first one in 37 years where I was not with a husband or children. I had come here on a whim with a new girlfriend. I told her I'd always wanted to go, and now for the first time in my life, I could make the decision without checking with anyone else. I was willing to make the eight hour drive alone if I had to, but she was able to go with me.

Doreen Virtue, the Angel Lady and prolific author, was on the stage. Dressed in white, long hair flowing, she looked like an angel herself. After speaking for about a half hour, she announced to the audience that she would do some readings. Immediately, hands flew up all over the place, and she called on those whom had deceased ancestors waiting in line to get messages to their loved ones.

Suddenly, she interrupted the reading she was giving to a woman in the third row and said, "Wait, I've got a message for a woman over there," pointing in my direction. That's when I knew something special was about to happen.

Doreen announced, "The Virgin Mary and Archangel Gabriel are here to tell you to write that book. They say you know who you are...where are you?"

As I said, I had been feeling the urge to write another book. I had also been feeling the presence of Virgin Mary and Mary Magdalene at my side. And yes, I thought perhaps this book was for women. But hey, I thought to myself, *look at all the hands up.* I guess there are a lot of us who want to write books! Surprise! Everyone has a book in them, right?

Still scanning the audience, Doreen continued, relaying the message from the Virgin Mary: "This woman has to write this book...it will empower women and heal children." And truthfully, the more she spoke, although other women were raising their hands around me hoping it was them Doreen was talking to, I knew it was me. I had already felt the presence of the Virgin and Mary Magdalene, visiting me and planting the seed for my next book.

Something shy inside of me said *oh my God, she's talking to me.* The Virgin, Jesus, and Mary Magdalene had come to me many times in meditation. I'm not a religious person, but I am spiritual. And I'd been going through the worst trauma of my life, so my need for my trio, as I like to call them, was pretty great.

Doreen went on to describe "the" woman—brown hair with streaks of gold. "You know who you are," she said. I shrank in my chair as Doreen pointed in my direction. Mind you, I'm among twenty-five hundred people! My friend stood up thinking it was her Doreen was talking about. "No, not you," Doreen gestured, "the lady sitting beside you."

What... me? My inner voice responded.

I stood, and Doreen said, "Yes, you."

Wow! I felt so exposed, so shy...so *what? Seen?* Yup, that's it. The angels were seeing me. Honestly, that felt pretty damn good!

I stood there nervously as they handed me a mic. "You know what they are saying to me, don't you?" Doreen said.

"Yes," I replied, "but for the life of me, I don't know what this book is about."

Her answer from the angels was to just sit down and write— it will come.

Well, that was all very cool. I mean, what are the odds? But, when two days later my chiropractor, also a healer, said, "Do you like to travel? Because I just saw you on a stage talking about a book you'd written," I knew

I'd just gotten my second command. The third came the next day as I pulled an Archangel card from one of Doreen's Angel Card decks I'd purchased. In response to the question "What I am supposed to do with my life," the card said:

"Write that book."

And just in case I somehow still didn't get the message—for good measure the same day, I received an email advertisement about an upcoming workshop, and the banner said...wait for it..."Write the Damn Book."

How many times have you felt that there was something special you were called here to do, and then felt it was just too egotistical to believe?—or maybe too scary to attempt or even understand...or perhaps just too big to allow. I know. I know! I've felt the same way. But far too many lives have been cracked open, hearts broken, and beliefs shattered for these experiences to have no meaning. I know the time has come for us to give birth to our own inner butterfly. But remember when she first emerges, her body is swollen, her wings damp. The struggle out of the cocoon is what squeezes the excess water from her body, much like we must squeeze out the last refuges of our old life. Her damp wings must have time to dry, stretch, and be infused with new blood before she can take flight, just as we must be infused with new understandings, new world views, and new dreams—all inspired by our soul's journey to live out our mission and our highest potential.

I invite you to come along with me, listen as I share my story knowing that yours may be similar. Let's explore our feelings, our pain, our needs, our journey through the time of "the unknown," expecting that we will find our answers and lighten our load. We will not only survive, but thrive. We will create the life we really want and deserve because we will come to know ourselves in a way we have never known. We will fall in love, perhaps for the first time, with the person most important to us—the one that is there always in every second of every day, through a lifetime of yes's and no's, the one that speaks in our dreams and takes action in our waking moments, the one we cannot get away from, whose constant chatter is mainly between our ears—who right now is demanding our attention saying, "Come on! This is our life! Let's start living!"

It's time to reclaim ourselves, to live authentic, connected, and empowered lives no matter our circumstances. And to do so, we must shed those tears, scream our hearts out, dig deep into our wound and disinfect it with gentleness. We must accept and forgive ourselves, acknowledge our fears, speak to our greatness, and embrace our flaws. We must be careful not to fall in love too quickly. Facing into our pain, we must be cautious of false infatuations that burn out quickly. Instead, let's fall in love slowly, gently, almost with a shyness that allows space for reflection and contemplation. This kind of love deepens, creates a foundation of strength, and outlasts any challenge we may face. It's the kind of love we give a friend as we come to know them over time, trusting them, learning from them, and accepting them just the way they are.

My story is an old one really—full of betrayal, abandonment, fear, loss, grief, anger, denial, and more. But now on the other side of healing, I am changed. I am no longer the woman I was when I went through this experience. I look back at who I used to be and feel nothing but compassion and empathy for that me because I know that she had no idea where she was going, who she was becoming, and what her life would be like, once she made it to the other side. This is the story of transformation: deep, real, painful, and necessary for our soul to fulfill this gift of life. And it all starts with crisis, with transitions. I began this book six years ago and wrote what I was experiencing as it was happening. At the beginning, there was a lot of pain as you will read. And I know you will relate. I will take you with me as time went on and months became years, as I began to heal, move through my experience, re-claim my soul, and re-invent my life.

You will see, in real time, the story of my transmutation. Let yourself feel the feelings alongside me. And as you read, I invite you to write about your journey too. If perhaps you are in the throes of pain right now, I hope that my sharing will help you see the light at the end of the tunnel. I know that what you are going through right now, painful as it is, will be the catalyst you need to become the butterfly you came here to be...it's your time to spread your wings and fly!

CONTENTS

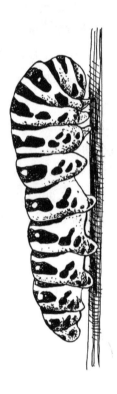

PART I

THE CATERPILLAR...
THE ENDING

As the caterpillar, we gather experiences, filling ourselves up until we are filled to capacity. We cannot grow anymore without the process of transformation. Our old beliefs, old stories, and old experiences no longer sustain the inner longing for who we are to become. And so an ending comes. That ending is a crisis of some kind, forcing us to grow beyond our own capacity. We can resist it, and sometimes do, for quite a while. But that resistance becomes more painful over time until we finally succumb. We cannot continue as we were.

THE DESCENT INTO THE DARK NIGHT

It's 3 o'clock in the morning, and I can't sleep. Lately, that's been a common theme. I take my melatonin to relax, then lie down under my cozy comforter, and my mind begins to spin. My body is flooded with anxiety and fear. No matter how many times I tell myself to breath, relax, change the subject, imagine butterflies—my thoughts keep coming back to all the "what ifs" and "if onlys."

I'm here, writing to you and wondering if you too are up in the middle of the night, alone with your feelings and no way to resolve them. The nights do sometimes feel very long, don't they? As your story plays like a bad movie over and over in your mind, perhaps in sharing my story, I will distract you enough that you may go back to bed with a better feeling than the one that drove you to the kitchen for a cup of tea.

Where do I begin?

I am a fifty-seven year old woman starting over again. How many of you can say the same thing? I've lived a life full of ups and downs, easy and tough times, joy and sorrow. I've worked hard all my life—done the "right thing," as Dr. Laura would say. I've loved and lost. I've been poor and what some would call rich and then poor again. I've prayed. I've cried. I've laughed. And like so many, I have had experiences that broadened my perspective, taught me about myself, and tested my courage.

And yet, here I am in a place I never expected to be. What was my expectation? Probably similar to every girl's dream. I expected after a lifetime of working that I'd have money in the bank, be at the top of my game in my career, retirement funds amassed, a home that my children and grandchildren would come to on holidays, and a man I adored and could grow old with.

Instead...

I lost my house and my retirement. My children, bless their hearts, have yet to give me grandchildren, my career is on hold as I deal with the emotional turmoil of so many losses, and the man I married had an affair with my best friend and turned out to be a complete stranger. My whole life feels like a lie right now. Everything I thought I knew, everything I thought I was...gone.

Once I had a man I loved: one I believed to be my soulmate; one with whom I shared my joys, my fears, my dreams, and my pain; one I tried so very hard to understand, to accept, to support; one I gave up many things for in order to keep a marriage through thick and thin. Gone.

Once I had a best friend who was like a sister to me: the person I shared my secrets with; the one who I'd run to with my pain and laugh with at the hardest of times; the one I trusted with my innermost emotions. Gone.

Once I had friends I shared myself with: a whole community that I called home, a village of support, fun and play; people I thought would always be there. Gone.

Once I had a beautiful house: one I decorated with love; one I entertained my family and friends in; one I took pride in; one filled with memories, good and bad. Gone.

Once I had money enough to travel, buy whatever I wanted, give to others in need, feel secure, save for retirement, and create fun adventures. Gone.

I am a stranger in a new land—a stranger to others and a stranger to myself. All the things I identified with, the people that I aligned with, the way I spent my days, even the work I loved, feels alien to me right now. My body too feels wrong in some way. My hair doesn't curl as it used to. My face has a line that looks like a tear falling from the corner of my eye, which was not there before my life fell apart. My smile is tired. My energy is drained. And I feel anxiety every time the phone rings. Sleeping only comes after a few hours of crying.

I am lost. I spend hours in my head playing out scenarios that I can't be sure occurred, hearing words said and unsaid. I spend one minute pleading, the next ranting. Honestly, I feel a little crazy at times.

And the weather...oh, how it matches my mood. It rains almost every day. I feel the angels are crying too. I wonder...are they crying with me? For me? Yes, I'm a little crazy I think. When your life changes in an instant,

I think it's okay to go a little crazy. You fall into the depths of your own shadow. None of the coping mechanisms work. You can no longer pretend it all away. I'm probably really depressing you right now! Or maybe you are right there with me: feeling the feelings, understanding all too well what I am describing.

I've spent my life working hard, loving openly, finding courage in the face of daunting challenges. I've amassed many skills. I've grown. I've shed some skins and grown some more. And yet, I feel stripped of it all. I am bare in this experience. I have no vantage point from which to exercise my old ways. Nothing works the way it used to. I am in the dark and can't find the light switch. I have come into the biggest crisis of self I have ever experienced. Perhaps you have entered this stage of the life of the caterpillar too: when there is no longer room to grow within our current life; when the only choice is to allow the transformation, to die a kind of death to the life we had in order to continue to grow. This is "the dark night of the soul" poets have talked about.

But they also talk about the light at the end of the tunnel. And that's what I'm searching for, hoping for, waiting for. I tell myself, "Be brave...I know it's there."

INSIGHTS:

When we step into the dark night of the soul, what makes it dark is not the experiences we've suffered. It's the realization that we no longer can identify ourselves through our outer life situations. All those personas we had molded ourselves into no longer support us. Safety is gone. Our rational mind can tell us to fight back, pick a new action, focus on something other than our pain. But the truth is our emotional mind is incapable of doing that. The pain is too visceral and cuts so deep. The most common feeling under the anger is helplessness and a lack of safety. Isolation fills the space where our lives used to be. Nothing can hold our attention very long, and every action we consider leads us back to the place of "not knowing" who we are anymore. And all we can do is be with the feelings. Although it may feel overwhelming—like the tears will not stop, like the pain will cut you in half—the truth is our bodies will take care of us if we let them. Our system is wired to shift the emotion when the heart is racing too much, when the breath is too shallow to sustain consciousness, when the muscles aren't being used to run. And so…I know that if I try to suppress, to deflect, to deny, to run away, I will never get through these feelings.

Did you know that studies show that 95% of our population will experience a betrayal at some point in our lives? It may be a betrayal with a spouse, a friend, a colleague, an employer, an employee, or even our own bodies. Betrayal is a broken spoken or unspoken promise, agreement or expectation. The severity of the pain is in direct proportion to the closeness of the relationship and the promise made. So great is this pain, psychologists today have named it "betrayal trauma." It is very similar to the symptoms of Post-Traumatic Stress Disorder. It's the breakdown of your worldview, your confidence, your sense of safety, your sense of self, and your ability to trust yourself or others. It really is one of the most difficult things to go through because, in the end, someone chose to betray you in some way. You feel devalued, unimportant, invisible.

And typically, betrayal is at the root of almost all transitions. One aspect that you will eventually come to understand as you work through this pain is how often you betrayed, abandoned and minimized yourself. To get through this, we must be kind to ourselves.

Remember children facing an angry parent or teacher will evade the truth when they feel shamed or blamed. We need to make space for the tender part of ourselves in order to feel free to explore our truths. The kindness I am giving myself allows me to be truly honest with myself, perhaps for the first time. Living an authentic life means we have to be real with ourselves first. So I invite you to talk with a counselor or trusted friend, have a conversation with yourself in the mirror, or journal your thoughts. These are ways in which we can "be" with the feelings and not act on them. And at this stage—in this place of darkness—this is the first step to an authentic life.

GONE IN AN INSTANT

My husband of 18 years was having an affair with my best friend. She was my friend for 24 years. Our children grew up together, and her family had been my surrogate family for just as long. She was and still is married to a wonderful guy. The affair ended when I found out, so did the friendship.

I'm not the first woman to be betrayed in this way, and unfortunately, I'm sure I won't be the last. I will say that I've met dozens of women, both in and out of my counseling practice, who have gone through the horrific pain of betrayal and am disheartened at how long it seems to take to heal from it. I can understand why though. It is because those who betrayed you had a choice to do something different, and they didn't. Dealing with the feeling that you did not "matter" at all to someone you loved is hard to get past. You feel discarded, like the trash. Invalidated and invisible, part of you wonders what you could possibly have done to deserve this.

Please understand this is not the whole story, and it's only the beginning of the ending. But it was when I began the descent into the "dark night of the soul." It was a life changing event. The infidelity didn't end my marriage initially; it simply served as a way to open my eyes to the truth about my life. That truth was...my life with this man was all based on lies. You see it wasn't just that he had an affair, and that it was also with my best friend. It took more than a year away from constant interaction with him for me to realize that I was suffering not only from the betrayal, but from years of emotional abuse.

And the worst part about it all was that I allowed it, not consciously, of course, but because of two inner deficiencies. I, like so many others, really didn't know how to love myself and had no idea how to live from my own personal power.

I remember the day my life unraveled like it was yesterday. It imploded without warning, in a split second, and I fell through the looking glass into a world that made no sense.

As I lay on the bathroom floor crying, the thing that ran through my head was, "He doesn't love me. He doesn't love me. He doesn't love me!" Of course there were a lot more things that kept popping in-between, things like: "It can't be true"; "How could they do this to me"; "I hate them both"; "I want to die." The list goes on. In one day, everything I thought was true turned out to be a lie. The two people I trusted most had completely destroyed me.

I later found out from other women who'd had similar experiences that they didn't get out of bed for weeks. That, in most cases, it took months before they shared the truth about their marriage to their family and friends, likely contributing to the prolonged pain they experienced. They let the behaviors of others become their own shame.

I didn't do that. I'm not sure why exactly. Perhaps it is because I've always been a survivor. But hours after the lights went out in my world and from within the black hole into which I had descended, I reached out immediately to my family, who came to my rescue within a day of the discovery: my mom, my sister, my brother, and their families, as well as my four adult kids. Everyone was in shock and wanting to help me. They were there holding me when I needed holding, listening to my wails of sorrow, watching while I ranted with rage, and of course, trying to make me eat. That one didn't work. I'd lost my appetite for everything and lost 10 pounds in 10 days. Now that's one hell of a crash diet!

I also reached out to the world that supported me. Yup, it's funny to say, but I did what so many have done when momentous things happened in their lives—I got on Facebook!

And this is what I posted:

"My heart is broken; I rage inside. The tears flow unannounced. My body shakes uncontrollably and sleep runs away from this roaring tide of emotion. Betrayal has slithered into my life while I lay basking in what I believed to be love. But I will not be defined by the actions of others. They cannot make me something I am not to soothe their guilt, to make themselves right. I will be neither their victim, nor their villain. And too, a hero I will not be. I will let my pain move through me like blue crystal water rather than jagged glass resisting the journey. And I will eventually find sleep and peace. I will become more. I will be my own greatness. I will live by my own internal compass. I will act from the greatest part of myself and be still with the weakest part giving her time to heal. I will not turn my back on love just because it hurts. I will embrace it instead with open arms, knowing I will love again."

I've been through so many phases since I wrote that on my Fan page. I wanted so much to believe then that I could somehow make this all go away. As much as I wanted to convince myself I was strong enough to see this through, I also couldn't believe it was happening. I'd fluctuate from denial to despair. I tried to tell myself that this event might be the catalyst that would save my marriage, while another part of me persuaded, "Run Forest Run!"

I remember the moments in that first week when the family sat around talking and laughing while I cried in the next room. It drove me crazy. How could life continue on normally when nothing was normal in mine? I felt as if I was in *The Twilight Zone*, and some alien invaders had taken over. This just can't be true! It was like my life had been divided into two parts: the memories of my husband and best friend and who I thought they were to me before this moment, and then after the discovery, the present, where they became absolute strangers to me.

He was my husband and partner, someone who I thought loved me, stood by me and wanted me. Yet he'd given his love, time, energy and attention to another woman while I waited for him at home.

She was my best friend, the one who I'd run to and share my deepest feelings with. She'd used those intimate conversations to satisfy her own ego.

The worst part of all was that during any other traumatic time in my life, these were the two people I'd turn to for comfort and advice. This is who I'd share my pain with and believed they would help me through. But I couldn't go to them now could I?

The realization of that truth was what made me feel like I was in a bottomless pit: dark, scary, and with no tethered rope to help me out. Honestly, there were just no words to adequately express the sheer terror of it all. I felt it so deeply until I couldn't breathe anymore; then I would become numb, feel nothing, and drop into bed in a fitful sleep, only to wake up the next day and find the nightmare was real.

It's been a year since the betrayal, and I still live with the shock of it. It still surprises me. Over this last year, I have moved twice, gotten back together with him, left him, gotten back together with him again, and finally divorced him. Now family and friends have returned to their normal lives, as they should. They call and check in, but they only want to hear that I'm okay, that I'm moving forward, that I've put the past behind me. So, I just puff up my feathers, put on a smile and say, "Yes, I'm great," when I'm really not.

As I write that, it seems so simple—just a short

chapter in my life. But it wasn't simple. Every day was filled with tremors, little earthquakes that rocked my world. You know what that's like, don't you? You've been there. Maybe your husband didn't have an affair. Maybe that's not what catapulted you into a reality you didn't know existed. But something happened, something big that altered your reality: a reality in which you gave your heart and soul only to find out that your love was played against you in the most insidious ways, one in which crazy-making behaviors seemed normal. You were told so many lies you couldn't even recognize the truth. You felt constant blame coming at you and took it on to make peace, and you found yourself walking on eggshells because you didn't want to make waves.

That was what my marriage had become in the last ten years. Now thinking back and re-reading my years of journals, I know the writing was on the wall from the beginning. I just didn't want to see it. I kept myself busy building companies, raising kids, creating fun, so that I could keep the marriage, not realizing how much of myself I was giving away. But others saw it and told me many times that I was slowly dying.

There were many times after horrible fights that I did think about leaving. I was living with someone that would change from day-to-day before my eyes. One minute he'd be civil, the next, angry. Counseling didn't help because he wouldn't go long enough to figure out what we could do to make things better. Every conversation would begin with him rolling his eyes at me, a sure sign of contempt.

My stress level was so high that my body was rebelling. I was on the brink of diabetes with constant pain in my joints and a general malaise that I couldn't quite identify. I began to believe what my friends told me, that I was slowly dying, but I just couldn't leave. Every time I would get close, he'd shift for a few days—be kinder, more loving—and I'd think okay, we can make this work. All I have to do is be patient, stay out of his way, and be as loving as I could.

That's the life I lived before the affair. But somehow, while he was having the affair behind my back, life seemed better: less anger, fewer arguments, a little more fun. He even told his son, only two weeks before the truth about his affair came out, that we had been happier and more in love than we'd been in years. Of course now I know why that was true for him. He was betraying me right under my nose, carrying on the affair in front of customers and employees of our business, who he'd already primed to feel sorry for him by telling them lies about how horrible I was. He was even texting her while I sat next to him.

There are really no words to describe what I felt when all this came to light. I stood in my kitchen and felt like someone had just punched me in the stomach. My breath was literally knocked out of me. For several minutes, I didn't know who I was or where I was. Reality shimmered, twisted, became fuzzy, and I was catapulted into the dark. How could this be? Who is this man... certainly not my husband? He could never do this to me! Not in a million years! Like I said, he became a stranger, my worst nightmare. This was the beginning of the end, not only of my marriage but of the life I'd been living.

Insights:

One of the biggest mistakes women make when they have been badly hurt, betrayed, or injured in some way is to hide their pain. We have been so programmed that other people's feelings are more important than our own, that to share makes us a victim, and being a victim makes us feel shame. Working with others and through my own experience, I know for sure that getting support right away can make a huge difference in the amount of time it takes to move through this pain. It's not about finding people to feel sorry for you...it's about finding people who can quietly remind you of who you really are under this sadness and anger. You need someone who will remind you to eat, hold you while you cry, show you the kindness you need right now because YOU won't be kind with yourself at this point. You will take on the full responsibility of what has happened because that is what most of us have been conditioned to do.

We don't realize sometimes how much we close our eyes to the things that are right in front of us. In doing so, it's easy to feel blindsided, that you had no idea...that you actually thought things were getting better. But I know now that the signs were there. The innuendos are quite obvious when looking back with 20/20 vision. This is the point where we must be careful not to beat ourselves up too badly. We didn't see what we weren't ready to deal with. I often asked myself what I would have done had I found out earlier, if I'd seen the actual texts, if I confronted the distant behavior. These thoughts can be dangerous. This is when we can do more damage to ourselves than was done to us. So when you have those thoughts—the "what ifs" and the "if onlys"—this is the time to treat yourself like you would a child, tenderly and with kindness. Soothe those thoughts, put them to bed with warm milk. The time will come to confront them. But it's not now. Now be gentle with yourself.

Spinning the Cocoon

I haven't consciously chosen this journey, but deep inside there is a part of me, perhaps it is my higher self—— the soul witness—whatever you want to call it, that knows the ending of my marriage had to come. I still needed answers, as wanting understanding is part of my nature. Perhaps it is yours too.

I want you to know that it took a long time for me to accept the truth about my marriage. I wanted to believe that this bad dream could be changed, and from this pain, I could fix whatever was wrong and make it right again. After all, I was a counselor. I had helped many couples come back and find each other after heartbreak. I told myself that his attitude toward me over the years was just a symptom of his own fear and lack of esteem.

I always knew he was selfish. I made excuses for his lack of empathy, for his criticism of others, for his inability to accept responsibility for his actions. I wanted to believe that even though his behaviors and words were hurtful, damaging, and abusive, in the depths of his soul, there had to be goodness and light. Call me naïve, but that's how I saw everyone. But I now understand that although on a soul level we are all love and light, many choose to express their humanness, in certain lifetimes, as anything but. And so after several years and many, many painful experiences, I have come to accept the truth about the man I married, although I still have a hard time reconciling the image of the man I fell in love with the person I know him to be today.

Now before you start thinking, "Wow, this woman is a saint! She really moves through this crap fast!" Let me just say...NO. I have those moments of clarity when I know, despite the horror and meanness, there still is good. But though I write it here for you to see, it really is just a fleeting thought. I'm not quite ready to embrace it yet. I still fluctuate and go back to..."How did that happen?"

It's a question that still keeps me up at night. Yet I know how. He was charming and said all the right things. On our first date, we kissed passionately for four hours straight while he said things like: "I've never met anyone like you," and "Where have you been all my life?" Though he'd had two unsuccessful marriages, he told me he was still interested in marriage and loved kids.

Within five days, we were practically living together. It makes sense now as I look back at it since he was renting a room from a couple and had no place of his own. He had creditors after him and owned nothing but a jeep. He so easily explained that it was *all* his ex-wife's fault. She was the crazy, mean bitch, and he had made sure that everyone knew it. Of course I believed him then, why wouldn't I? I've only now had the opportunity to talk with her and confirm that most of what he told me was a lie. She even revealed how surprised she was when she learned we were getting married because he was still calling her at the time and sending her love notes asking to get back together. She felt betrayed by me! Who knew! Part of me wished that I'd talked to her way back when, but I knew I probably wouldn't have believed her any more than his next conquest will believe me.

Playing the victim and feeding on the pity of others is what these kinds of men do. They manipulate you through your empathy and look for your vulnerability. They shower you with affection, play the "nice guy" until they know they've got you. Then, they simply test the water by pulling back or saying some small snide remark, and you immediately wonder, "What have I done?" That's when they know for sure they are in control, right? — that they have their conquest hooked and can behave however they want. Unfortunately for women like us, we didn't know we were in a game of cat and mouse, and we certainly didn't know the rules. And then, there we are beating ourselves up over it. Could that be the source of our anxiety and fear, what haunts us when we try to sleep—all the "should haves"?

I should have known when he stood me up on our third date because he decided to drink with a buddy instead of meet me that I was really not that important to him, and I'd always come last. I should have known when he'd keep me waiting for hours that my feelings meant nothing to him. I should have known when he would criticize me and tell me I was crazy when I was upset about something he did that he was incapable of empathy. I should have known when things went wrong and he always blamed everyone else that he never took responsibility for his actions... or when he hid a credit card from me for over a year and lied, that there were more lies I had yet to discover... or when he didn't show up at the Emergency Room for two hours as I was lying there possibly having a heart attack that he really didn't care if I lived or died. Oh yes, I should have known.

But I didn't. Why? Because I thought he loved me! Right? He told me I was the best thing that ever happened to him. The problem was that what he loved was what I had, not who I was. He loved that I had a house which I used to pay off his debts and get rid of the creditors knocking down his door. And of course, I put him on the title without him giving me a dime. He loved that I had children and a family that would make him appear respectable and raise his status higher because he was "the good guy" who took on a woman with four children. He actually said that to me: "You're lucky I came along because what man would marry a woman with four kids?"

He loved that I was smart and could handle the finances, resolve problems for him, and ultimately, start and run a two million dollar company which he benefited from while he played golf and pretended to be busy at his desk. Oh yes, he loved me for what I could do for him, give to him... make of him.

I didn't see the signs along the way, the signs that he was untrustworthy, a pathological liar who never took responsibility for anything and blamed others for everything that was wrong. I never noticed that he never really apologized after hurting me without somehow insinuating that it was my fault. And I took it all. For eighteen years, I gave this man everything I had—my home, my money, my support, my care, and my love. And more importantly, I gave him my self-respect, my power, my intuition, and in the end, my sanity.

Now I can blame him, and I do for all the lies, the cheating, the total disregard for my feelings, my needs, and my safety. I blame him for his lack of empathy, his selfishness, his cruelty and his lack of remorse. I now know what he's capable of, but only the people closest to him, namely a wife—and I was his third—would ever be able to see who he really is. And he doesn't keep us for very long. I was the longest relationship he'd ever had and hopefully ever will because he nearly destroyed me, and I know he'll do it again to some other unsuspecting woman. I am now the crazy bitch, alongside his other ex-wife.

But I can't ultimately blame him for what I accepted from him. Some would say that I always had a choice to leave, and I thought of doing that many times, but didn't. I stayed, begged for counseling, kept out of his way, gave him complete control, and supported him and his decisions. I continued to trust him, even though he betrayed that trust constantly. That was my bad, which

I can take responsibility for. Even now I can see that, though I am still not sure why. Why would a woman who appears to have a healthy sense of self and know her capabilities take that kind of treatment? Ugh! I wish I knew, and maybe that's part of this journey.

Trust is such a sacred thing we offer others. I truly believe that. It is greater even than love. When we trust another, we are affirming that we feel safe with them because we feel they have our best interests in mind, and we matter to them. Trust. It's BIG! It's right up there with FAITH. It's something intangible, and yet, we sense its absence when we feel afraid, cautious, and timid. Without it, we hold ourselves back from giving completely, from opening our hearts, from being fully ourselves and dropping the masks we learn to wear.

So betrayal of trust, on any level, is to me the greatest harm we can do to another person. It is the hardest thing to come back from because we don't only learn to distrust those who hurt us, we also begin to distrust ourselves on a very deep level. We feel so invalidated when we realize we don't matter at all to someone that was so important to us. We feel separate, which is the most painful of psychic wounds. From the moment we are born, we separate spiritually from our Source and quite literally from our mother. We spend a lifetime creating, longing for, and doing everything we can in an attempt to regain that feeling of oneness. We want more than anything to belong. That is why we stay in situations, relationships, jobs, and careers sometimes longer than we should. And that is why betrayal is the hardest thing to heal from because in the end, we betrayed ourselves too.

While the unraveling of my marriage happened over a two-year period, as I further process my journey, I've come to realize how I had been living with constant anxiety for most of my marriage. I will be sharing some of the story to give you context so that you can perhaps identify with me and maybe recognize some truth about your own life. However, this book isn't just about what happened in the past. It is about what is happening for me now in those quiet moments when I find a way to reclaim my soul. For that is what must happen, right? We can't let our lives be defined by what others have done to us. We were "somebody" before we entered the cocoon, before we collapsed into the void, the nothingness of ourselves, and we will be "somebody" again!

Still for now, as I sit here and the dawn is breaking over the horizon, the birds have started their morning calls; I have come to understand three reasons about how this ending crept into my life unannounced.

One is that it is unimaginable to someone with a heart and a conscious that there really are people out there who can hurt you so badly. The problem is what they do, as you well know, is not obvious. It's riddled with some truth, which is the best way to conceal a lie. What they do is so strategic, we don't even know what's happening until it's too late. We become conditioned to put them first, to believe their lies, to think the problem is us. In other words, we are emotionally abused on so many levels we become the frog in slowly-boiling water, comfortably accepting the heat until it kills us before we know what is happening.

The second reason is because we don't even realize how they have worked to garner support against us. While we defend their inconsiderate actions, justify their selfishness, and stand by their decisions even though the effect may be disastrous for us, they are building their camp and readying for their departure to greener pastures. Others may notice some poor behaviors or bad choices, but they have conditioned these people to believe they are the victims so others close their eyes and remind themselves it's none of their business, condoning behavior through their silence they would never want done to themselves. Isn't that how it is with most of what we all see and abhor? But I believe that the world will not change, that families will continue to perpetuate dysfunction and abuse because no one says "enough."

Yes, it is not our place to judge or change what another is doing. I can't help wondering what would happen if those that saw and heard stood up and simply said: "I don't condone what you are doing, and I will not be a part of your life, your business, or your community while you hurt others." Perhaps these abusers would not end up destroying families, becoming powerful businessmen who destroy economies while they line their pockets, or running countries and creating wars that destroy lives. I just wonder if perhaps we started at home, in our small lives, to simply stand up and say "no"—might we heal the children growing in these environments, and in doing so, might we actually heal the world? As I write this, I feel a strong sense that our evolution depends on our ability to face fear with love, not by closing our eyes, ears, and mouths to those things that have such a devastating impact on us and others. Instead we name that which is not love, own responsibility for what we witness, and lovingly say, "This is not okay, and I won't condone it anymore with silence."

The third and most important reason we stay and take it, doing everything we can to make it work even though there is a part of us that knows things will never change, is because we have forgotten who we are. We have "bought into" their story about us to some degree. We have decided that they are more important than we are. We have loved them more than we love ourselves.

Let's agree on two things. One is that we are all special—that we come here, do the best we can, and sometimes even more than that. The second is we can continue to grow, make mistakes, really screw up, lose our way...and still find our way back.

We still know there's more to this thing called life, that we are ever expanding, and we are dependent on one another to reach our full potential, that as much as it may hurt, as much as we'd like to escape, blame, and shame ourselves, we have an opportunity for greatness through this experience. WE can become *more* than what we believe ourselves to be.

We are always guided, whether we know it or not. You and I are the same. Perhaps the story lines are different and the characters we play unique. But no matter, we still feel the same things, the love for our family, the pain of defeat, the grief of loss, the anger of betrayal, the dedication to our work, the joy of making love, the sacrifices, the fight to survive…all of it. We are the same.

I have come to a place of knowing that the messages contained within are important. For healing to occur in this world, for a world filled with conscious people supporting each other and following their hearts' desires, it has to start with you and me. I truly believe that when we women heal our hearts, embrace our Divine Feminine power, and live authentic lives, the world will change. But we cannot heal in isolation. We cannot heal through blame and shame. We cannot be who we came here to be if we do not allow ourselves to feel our feelings. We must change from the inside out. That is what I'm doing. I know that is what it will take for you, too.

Maybe one woman's journey is truly the journey of all women. The Divine Feminine is ready to take her rightful place in this world, and we, her physical form, are ready to step up and claim our power—perhaps in doing so, we can make the world a better place.

INSIGHTS:

I don't know what happened to you. I don't know if you've been living with a narcissist or sociopath, an alcoholic, an abuser, suffered a great loss financially, been raped, or what has brought you to these pages, but if something is resonating with your heart, your pain, your situation...then let me just say, I understand. Our stories don't have to be exactly the same for us to have empathy and compassion for each other. I understand that those thoughts that keep you up at night, circle your brain while you are doing the dishes, infiltrate conversations with friends even though you are trying not to talk about it, and overlay so much of your daily routine, are really hard to control. You tell yourself to "Stop it...Just, STOP IT," but it's almost impossible. In the replaying of your story, you finally understand something you really don't want to see, but that is important for you to heal. Despite what we have gone through, what "he" has done to us, the saddest thing of all is that we know we have become the co-dependent enabler who allows the abuse to continue.

That's a huge, ugly pill to swallow and hard to forgive ourselves for, I know. But that's what we have to do. It's the only thing that will give us back our lives, resuscitate our joy, free up our hearts to love again, and ignite the passion we came to this planet with that is our unique gift to the world we live in. It's that simple!—and that difficult.

So hang in there. Write out your story. Add to it as I have, whenever you need to get it out of your head. Start reading from the beginning, the things you've written so far, before your write your next entry. There is something very healing about watching your thoughts slowly shift, noticing your feelings aren't as raw, sensing something inside beginning to transform. This is something that I experienced and found highly enlightening and therapeutic. You are basically holding your own hand, and that's the greatest gift you can give yourself.

As the Caterpillar Dies

I t's early morning after another fitful night of sleep. I sense I've had dreams, but they are like wisps of smoke. I make myself a cup of coffee, check my emails, and see this post by Elizabeth Gilbert on Facebook in which she describes how devastating it is to go through betrayal. She writes of how lost we feel, how unrecognizable our life becomes, how it is never a choice, but rather something that just happens to us, and how this is the beginning of the hero's journey Joseph Campbell refers to as the "dark night of the soul." She explains that we must enter the void—the unknown—and will eventually find peace through understanding this event, maybe even coming to think of it as a blessing. I love her as an author and love that she is my muse today.

So, this is the promise of our challenge, even if we don't feel it or sense it right now.

My journey is taking me into the void, the emptiness of "not knowing." It is a difficult place to be, but one I think you can probably relate to. From this place, I feel the stirrings of something deep inside. Something is demanding my attention—something I think other women also feel. I have met so many women whose story mirrors mine. I've seen and heard their pain, joined in the feeling of being stuck in one's story, unable to move forward. It's so easy to stay stuck in this place where nothing makes sense: where the future is dark and lonely and where survival mechanisms may make me feel better, but will not move me forward. So I'm here…in the void… in the unknown…OMG!

And I don't like it. I wonder what I will change into, how much of the me that I've been experiencing these last few years will survive. How will the change bring about a better life? Right now, it all eludes me. I pray a lot for a peaceful heart, for the tears to stop, for a miracle to happen. My mind and heart is still filled with the sense of loss that runs so deep I am empty. I wonder was I really ever happy? I thought I was. But looking back at those times fills me with such anguish and so many regrets, I have to make myself stop before I completely lose track of what's real for me now. Still I find myself re-reading old journals to try to pinpoint when it all went wrong, figure out what was true and what wasn't, and create a timeline of understanding for events that occurred in hopes of finding clues I missed.

Keeping journals is an important ritual for me. Occasionally, my spirit guides will speak to me as I write. The other day, I found this entry dated only eight months before my husband embarked on his affair. While I haven't always been so sure my channeling was actually my guides' voices speaking and not my own mind playing tricks on me, the entry was interesting and profound. This is what I'd written:

We are here with you always. No reason to fear us. We are one with you dear one. We have always been and will always be. Indeed the time has come for all mankind to change, to grow, to become one in the All-ness. This you have known for quite a while. Like the caterpillar in the cocoon, you have been going through your own transmutation. And it is now time to emerge to the Butterfly in you. We sense that you are ready, even though you may not think so. You have a mission to accomplish, as do so many others like you. You will see your full potential, and you must not fear your own greatness. For when you stand full in your highest potential, you experience pure joy. Your heart is completely open, and you are prepared to give your all. This is the example for others who doubt. This is what they see and what truly inspires them. And that is all that is needed. Only be open, aware, and ready for the opportunities that come each day to share your message—our message—to help others come home to their true nature, to know themselves fully, to live and forgive each other and themselves, to be kind to themselves, as you have so eloquently been telling them unknowingly for years. It will all become clearer to you each day. You need only be awake, keep your heart open, trust the process, and remember always, our dear, that you are loved. You are love. You are part of the oneness of the All-ness. You are never alone. We love you and are happy to have this way of communicating. We look forward to this dialogue and will be available at this time, the quiet time—the power hour—to continue this conversation. For now, what is important to reiterate again is that you are emerging—you are becoming. You are transmuting, ever changing, expanding into the wholeness of the oneness that is part of the All-ness. And so it is.

I wish I could say that I did what they asked, that I continued to meet at the quiet time to channel more messages from Spirit, that I opened up to my knowing with ease and clarity. Unfortunately, that is not what happened. Instead, I got scared, and I closed down to what was really happening in my life.

Occasionally, I would get an intuitive hit that something wasn't right in my world. However, I'd quickly shut the message down to keep the peace and maintain the status quo, thereby delaying the transformation into what I was meant to be because my fear was so great—my fear of being alone, abandoned, and unloved. Oh, the irony. Although on the surface, I worked at being happy, keeping my vibration up, creating workshops, writing books, and meeting with amazing people, it would be only months after that channeled communication that the bricks to oblivion would be laid out--the destruction of my marriage, my world, my peace of mind.

So, now I see my caterpillar self must die. Compelled by life circumstances, I have come to a place where nothing is recognizable anymore. I tried. I tried to put my life back together again. I told myself he was going through a mid-life crisis, and I hadn't been as loving as I could be. I bought his excuses and his tears.

I had moved out of the home he had abandoned just four weeks after the affair came to light. I had found a sweet little cottage, put up my pictures, lit candles every night, sat in the hot tub and cried myself to sleep. All I could think of was how this wasn't what I wanted. I wanted my marriage back. I begged him to give us a chance, told him I wasn't ready to divorce him, and made myself believe that we could work this out.

At first, our time together was filled with sex, a powerful way to convince oneself that you are loved. I needed to feel close to him, to believe that the affair was just a symptom of our lack of connection. Truthfully, I needed to know I was still desirable because I felt so rejected. But after several months, the sex slowed down. He was once again distant. He never did anything to champion our marriage or show me that I really did matter to him. The slightest attention filled me with hope while the more common aloofness from him made me angry.

Over time, I began to truly be disgusted with myself and with his selfish antics. His continued attention to other women in the face of his betrayal was a sign that I was deluding myself—a sign I didn't want to see. I would get angry and tell him it was hard to rebuild trust when he continued to act as he was with other women. He often responded, "You will never forgive me." I was exasperated. How was I supposed to forgive him when he blatantly continued to hurt me?

I was trying so hard to put the pictures in my mind into a vault I couldn't open: trying so hard to fill the cracks of my broken heart with sex, fun, lightness; trying so hard to turn the volume down to my inner wisdom; trying so hard to pretend once again that we were happy. I cooked luscious meals, planned romantic interludes, stayed out of his way with the business, kept myself busy with my work, and once again, stuck my head in the sand.

Meanwhile, I was hearing from others the terrible things he was saying about me. I was told he had brought women to my home while I was out of town. I began noticing how his family and son were not treating me as the family member I'd been for eighteen years because of lies he'd told them to rationalize his affair. He had turned the tables on me once again making his affair somehow my fault. He blamed me for all his abhorrent behaviors.

One Saturday morning, we were having coffee when his phone rang. I could only hear his side of the conversation, but it was clear that he had made plans with some customer to go golfing the following day. I heard him say, "I'm sorry man, I can't. I have a church thing I have to go to," then hung up.

I sat there stunned. He never went to church. He hated it. But what I realized was how easily he lied to this man. It rolled out of his mouth without a second's pause. The truth was that he was working the following day. He always worked Sundays. My question was why tell the man a lie when the truth was just as good, or an even better reason, for not being able to meet?

When I asked him why he lied, he simply said, "I'm working tomorrow, so I can't golf." I said, "I know, so why tell him a lie?" His defensive response was, "What's the big deal? Why do you always make a big deal?"

"I'm just trying to understand why you would tell him you were going to church when you could have just told him you were working?" I replied.

"I don't get why you are upset about this. It has nothing to do with you anyway!" he yelled.

I think that was the moment when I finally saw I could never, ever trust a word this man told me. He truly was unable to differentiate a lie from the truth. He had no integrity, and if I stayed with him, neither would I.

Within days, I told him I wanted a divorce. I was done.

At that point, I finally looked at the books of the business we owned together to estimate its value for settlement purposes. That's when I found I was betrayed in ways that went past emotional heartache. This time there were things that threatened my financial security, all while we were going through bankruptcy, and he was telling me to get a job. More deception. I was devastated.

I kept quiet, planned my departure, came up with a settlement, said goodbye to the people that mattered to me, and set off to a new town. I left him exactly eighteen years to the day that we first met on a blind date. It was raining the whole way to my destination, but it was hard to see the rain outside through the tears running down my face.

I want so much for it all to be done, for this time to be over, for my mind, heart and life to be healed and transmuted into the potential I know I have within me—my own imaginal cells, the butterfly waiting inside. But for now, I must accept that all I've been through was part of my caterpillar life. It is more than the ending of a marriage right now. It is a time when I am feeding myself, outgrowing my shell, gorging again on the experiences necessary for my transmutation, my transformation. I think that's pretty cool, even though it hurts like hell. But the journey continues as it must, from one leaf to another, from one feeling to another, until I am compelled by something deep within me to create my cocoon. I love this metaphor. It gives me a sense of peace, and I hope it does the same for you. Spirit has a plan for me and has one for you too. We always have the choice to use our will to change, thwart, or delay Divine Order. That's what I did. But I do believe there is no punishment for that, only more information, more depths of understanding, more expansion. Yup, I like that.

I sense that the cocoon is complete. I have shed my last caterpillar skin. I have reached the capacity of growth in the life I was living. If I was going to grow anymore, I would have to dissolve into the soup of my existence and become. Become what? I am yet to know.

Insights:

When I left him, when I decided to leave the place I called home…that was the first step toward my healing. Sometimes we must change our environment in order to really begin the healing process. Proximity can keep us stuck in that vicious cycle of trying to maintain what we know, even though it hurts like hell. It took a lot of self-care, self-discipline and self-respect to make this move. Of course, I didn't recognize that at all. I just knew I couldn't keep doing what I was doing. I had chosen to leave my home of twenty-five years, the place I loved, and where I'd lived longer than anywhere else in my life. It was the place where I felt I belonged. Connection is a powerful need and elixir. But sometimes, we have to reach for a deeper connection than we can possibly get from the external world. We need to connect with our higher power—with God—with anything that feels bigger than ourselves. We also need to connect with the smallest part of ourselves, the one without a voice…the part that needs our attention and love.

I chose my new home because it was far away enough from him for me to sever the tie and feel safe, and it was close enough to go back to my kids and friends when I needed connection with them. I only knew three people in my new town. On an intuitive level, I knew it was time to be alone with myself—connecting. The only other thing I knew was it rained a lot. It suited me fine; the skies and my tears were in synch. The drive over the mountain was the longest and saddest drive I'd ever taken. I couldn't say then I was going home because I didn't know anymore where home was.

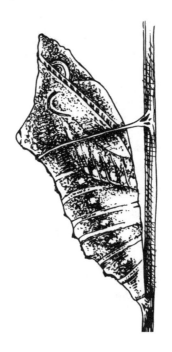

PART II

THE COCOON...
THE IN-BETWEEN

Like the caterpillar, we enter the time of in-between. We are in the chrysalis, or cocoon, a place where all that we were unravels to reveal who we might become. Most of us go there not by choice. We feel forced, compelled by external events or people. But I've come to understand that although some of that is true, the bigger truth is we participated in it, whether consciously or unconsciously, because our soul demanded it. Once in this place, this in-between, we are like newborns, vulnerable and innocent. We start to let go, accept the death of the old, and feel the urges of something new. It is a time of our own personal resurrection.

Dissolving into the Nothingness

Today, I felt like killing myself and not for the first time since my life fell apart. I know it's probably surprising that this is how I'm feeling today after what I wrote just a few days ago. But that's how it is on the road to transformation. I find myself in the throes of despair, and I let myself feel that. Then my mind steps in, trying to make sense of my feelings, attempting to ease my pain— to protect me. While I resist shutting down the feelings, I get glimpses of "what could be" once this ride is over. Today, I hit bottom… again. So I sit with it. I ache all over. I feel so alone, though I know there are so many who love me. But in this moment, this time of darkness, I feel adrift in the universe and killing myself sure seems like a good way to stop the feelings.

I'm sharing this with you because I know that you too feel that desperate to get away from the pain. You too feel the total isolation and hopelessness. And I bet these thoughts scare you as much as they scare me. Even though we have these thoughts, may even consider ways in which we could get the deed done, we are still here. There is something strong inside of us, something that won't let us give up. Or maybe we just can't do it to those we love and whom we know love us. We stop ourselves because we know the pain that makes us have these thoughts is transferred directly to the ones left behind who will be wondering for the rest of their lives how they could have saved us. Our beloved will be feeling that same desperation to understand, to make the pain of the loss stop, to somehow get past the horror and helplessness of it all.

So we don't do it! Right? I mean... I'm here. You're here. Let's keep it that way. But let's also talk about it. Letting it out, hearing your voice saying the words out loud triggers our most natural instinct, that human instinct to survive. I think when we speak the words fill the space around us, getting us in touch with reality in a different way than when we are keeping these thoughts inside and hidden. Trust me, I have worked with suicidal people, and when they choose to live, every one of them is happy they did.

When I was 16, my best friend's mom killed herself. She was a woman who survived the Holocaust. At 13, believing that her parents were dead, she escaped the concentration camp with her little sister in tow. From Poland, she crept through the night, stealing food and clothing along the way, until she managed to get through war- torn Europe and stowed away on a boat to America. Unbelievable, isn't it? Hard to imagine the courage it took—the stamina, the determination—to seek out

41

something she had no experience of, to do what I would say most adults could not do.

She somehow made a life for herself and her sister in America. Eventually, she found her parents and brought them to the States too. She got an education, married a nice Jewish boy, and became the mother of three great kids. To say she was strong would be an understatement. But there she was, at 45, after all she'd been through, and her strength failed her at her time of need. She took her life because her house was slipping down the hill, its foundation faulty, and knowing it would cost a lot to fix it, she didn't want money "wasted" on her. When the mind is trapped and the heart is broken, drastic choices don't seem so drastic, and rational thought is hard to reach.

We had just come home from school, and my friend lived down the block. After setting down my things, I heard a frantic knocking on the door. There was my friend, white as a sheet, yelling, "My mom is dead! She's dead...she's dead." *This is not funny.* I think to myself. *This can't be happening. What is she saying?*

She grabbed my hand and pulled me down the block, through her front door and into her parents' room, where I saw, for the first time, what a dead body looks like. Like her, I think I went into shock right away. It was like one of those dreams where you want to scream and you open your mouth, but nothing comes out.

The rest is a blur, except the tears. I watched my friend grow up in one day. She was no longer a sixteen year old discovering her first love. She was now mother to her siblings and caretaker of the household. And in that moment, I knew I could never, ever take my own life.

Until today...today, as I sit with my anguish, I feel powerless to change my circumstances, disconnected from the independent, intelligent and successful woman I used to be. I am lost, confused, helpless, tied-up in knots, chained to a life I don't want, and not yet happy to be freed from a life I never really had and never would have. I feel the hopelessness. I think about just letting go, slipping into a slumber I won't awake from, willing my body to just stop breathing. I imagine not feeling this pain anymore.... and then images of my family flash through my mind alongside the image of my childhood friend's mother—dead—and I stop these thoughts. To be honest, I feel a little angry that I just can't be selfish enough!

Sometimes I hear myself saying, "I wish he were dead" instead of living in my hometown showing off his new girlfriend, acting like our business is his alone, and getting "Atta Boy!" from all our employees, his friends and family. But then I feel bad, you know, because that is not who I am. Does that ever happen to you too? You find yourself thinking and feeling in a way that is foreign and get scared. You feel like you are losing your soul.

I feel isolated and alone. I walk out on my patio, and I can hear "life" around me: the birds are still singing; the neighbor mowing his lawn; the mailman delivering the mail. As people walk by, I scream in my head, "I'm here... help me...I need someone to tell me I matter." But no one hears that internal scream. No one knows the pain I'm in.

So I find a way to distract myself. I sit with my cigarettes—my only companion—and play solitaire on my ipad to drown out my own thoughts.

You understand how that feels, don't you? It is the feeling that you are completely alone: that no one gets how much you hurt, that everyone wants you to be okay. You know they love you, but you feel let down by them. They still have a life, while yours has been torn to shreds. I have a new understanding of Humpty Dumpty now, don't you?

It feels like our lives will never be put back together again, as if something is lost, and we can't find it because we are blind—a poor combination for seeing clearly the choices we may have. So you sit too, don't you? You might not smoke, but maybe you drink, or maybe you shop, or maybe you stay in bed all day...or maybe you look for love in all the wrong places.

And a part of you says, "What the hell has happened to me?" I ask: "Where did that woman go who raised four kids while working two jobs? Who was that lady who started a company from scratch and turned it into a two million dollar operation with a hundred employees? What happened to that girl who believed in people...in miracles...in possibilities?" Maybe your accomplishments aren't the same as mine, but you know that feeling of looking back at who you used to be—strong, confident, capable—and wondering where the hell did *that you* go!

In answer, a small voice in your head says, "I'm here... I'm here, I think."

Tired of hearing my own voice, I turn to others. My friend tells me to go into the void, to the depths where my answers can be found. But I feel I've already done that, and so I argue the point. *How far down can I go?* What if I can't get out? What if I'm there now? How will I know?

My daughter and mother try to remind me of who I am, what I'm capable of, and what I "should do" to take care of myself: eat well, sleep well, exercise, get counseling...take anti-depressants. Huh? They just don't get it. I've done all those things, and still, the feelings persist.

I can't find the energy. I feel no passion about anything. *"Oh my God,"* I realize, *"I am a VICTIM. I am!"* I've been hurt and abandoned by those I loved: him; her; his family, who claimed to love me for the past twenty years; friends; employees—all of them gone.

And round and round the mulberry bush I go. I don't know what to do except feel it. And when I get to that place as I have today, where escape from the pain looks like a one way street to Nowheresville, I remember the look on my best friend's face forty years ago, and I know I can't put others through unbearable pain by ending my life.

So, today I live. Instead of thinking about how to end my life, I write to you. I tell you of my despair and hope that as I share, you recognize your own thoughts and choose as I have.

Even as I write these words, I sense a new vibration in my body. One that others don't want to see, deal with, or explore any more than they did my "helplessness." It is one that moves me from despair to the inklings of the power I once knew. I begin to feel better as this new emotion slowly emerges. Yes, I actually feel some relief.

It starts with irritation with myself, annoyance with others, and then builds into ANGER. I wonder…can I go there? Is it okay to really feel it and know I won't become some bitter old woman out for revenge? I'm not sure I'm ready for this. I let a little out, enough to stop the boil inside. But it scares me and scares others, so I lower the heat for now.

Yet, I know that somewhere under my personal story, my pain, my stuckness, my fear, and yes, my anger is the woman I was born to be. A part of me wonders if all I've been through—all you're going through now—is part of some great tapestry that will ultimately transform us into more than who we used to be. If we allow it, that is, if we are willing to follow the thread to a new design. Yes, it requires taking stock of where we are, taking responsibility for our part of the journey, and being willing to imagine something new, something good, maybe even something great in our future.

I want to believe that. I have to believe that to go on. I have always believed that there are no accidents. Everything happens for a reason. And yes, I, on some level, whether conscious or unconscious, created this. Many have said this while I was sharing my pain. Not helpful, is it?—to be told that the *Law of Attraction* means you attracted this stuff in because on some level you were vibrating at that level of energy. It's not helpful either to have someone say, "Open your heart and begin to forgive," when your heart is so broken—broken wide open—into tiny shards that are sharp. I know they are only trying to be helpful, but what I need is to feel my feelings. And part of feeling them is sharing my story. I'm sure at some point I will accept my own responsibility in this mess I called my life, but for now...let me be. Let me feel. Don't hand me philosophy. Don't hand me platitudes. Don't hand me a mirror. Not yet. Please.

These are the thoughts I have. Right now, I'm at a crossroads and perhaps you are too. One path takes me round in circles, going nowhere while life passes me by. The other path is dark and scary, but through the overgrown trees, brambles and weeds, I see a light. I realize that our stories are a perspective of life, not life itself. I know what the old story is, but the new story hasn't begun to emerge. I know if I stay here too long, it never will. So even now, in this pain, I am determined. Why? Because what is true is that I am a survivor... always have been. I just don't want to *only* survive. I want to flourish.

I know the light in the distance is where my future lies. I know the woman I have the potential to be is in there somewhere, and I am going to find her! Are you willing to find yourself too?

INSIGHTS:

It is a very painful thing to watch someone give up on themselves, and suicide leaves families forever scarred. It is understandable that in the throes of pain and despair one might want it all to end. We really don't handle pain well, especially in this country.

It's not abnormal to feel alone during times of great transition; but remember, you are not. Reach out to a friend when it gets so bad you don't feel you can go on. Call a mentor, counselor, the Suicide Prevention Hope line…anyone. There is a better tomorrow.

Here is a question to ponder, one that has saved the lives of many I've worked with to get past the thoughts of death…

If I woke up tomorrow…and all this was behind me…the pain was suddenly gone…what would I see…what would I hear…what would I feel…what would I be doing? Let yourself truly go there, to that tomorrow, and notice all that's there—all that's possible—all that's new and shiny and pain free.

There is somewhere "beyond now." You are on your way there. The "you" that is becoming, that is being birthed through this betrayal, is so beautiful, radiant, strong and vulnerable, wise and intuitive, full of trust and ready to connect in an authentic and powerful way with a world that awaits your splendor…

So hang on!!!!! It's worth it.

An Italian Visitation

Wow! I'm in Italy. It is one of the most romantic places on the planet. I'm not here with a man! I'm here with a friend who went through the same betrayal experience as me.

She called one day and said, "Italy has been on my bucket list for years. I've planned this trip twice already and had to cancel it because the man I was going with broke up with me. I'm not going to do it again! Will you go with me?"

Unlike my friend, Italy was not on my bucket list, and spending five thousand dollars on myself seemed so outrageous. Besides, I was still in no mood for happiness, adventure, or fun. I was still feeling the anxiety in my body that years of constant tension can cause. But my children convinced me that I needed this distraction, that perhaps this could be the start of something new—and that at the very least, I deserved a "break today."

So I booked my flight and here we are. The great thing is that I don't have to pretend to have a good time with this friend. She knows all too well how I am feeling.

She has been tender and loving and has given me the space I needed.

We have seen it all, from one end of Italy to another: the riches and awe of the Vatican and Sistine Chapel; the gorgeous Amalfi coast; the ruins of Pompeii and the Colosseum; the art of Florence; the charm of walled cities with cobblestone roads; and the brilliant, ancient beauty of cathedrals. It has been my own special version of *Eat, Pray, Love*...only I haven't done any of those things.

I have had days where my mind could remain occupied by the sites and days when the sadness overlaid the beauty in front of me. Sometimes I engage in the laughter of others in our tour, while at other times their laughter makes me cringe. I wanted to immerse myself in the experience, yet I wanted to be left alone. You know how that is? To be honest, I'm feeling torn in so many directions. And I keep asking myself why am I here? What is it that I will learn?

Last week we went to the Vatican. As I stood in St. Peter's Square watching the people pay homage, the bells sung out the coming of the Pope. He apparently comes to a window and blesses the crowd on Sundays. I am not Catholic. And the Pope isn't my spiritual leader, but somehow, standing out there on that day, seeing and hearing the love coming from this man, albeit in Italian, something in me broke down. I offered my pain to God. I asked that I be given at least a reprieve from my pain. I was open to a miracle.

And then...one happened...

While in Florence, I had the inspiration to buy myself a ring. I wanted to adorn my wedding finger with a ring that would be a reminder to always stay committed to myself before anyone or anything else. Anyone who's been to Florence knows that this is the capital of jewelry. So I went from store to store seeing beautiful rings...all too big...all too gaudy...all not for me.

Then by chance, as a last ditch effort, I walked into a very tiny shop. And there it was...a small ring with a ruby in it. The ruby was ringed in silver, and the silver was ringed in gold. As I slipped it on my finger, a perfect fit, the sales lady said it was an antique and one of a kind. And it was $350 American dollars. I decided I'd had to think about it, which for me was a change. I've always been a woman who bought what she wanted without thinking about it. Why not? I had perfect credit! I could do like so many do—buy something even when I didn't have the cash.

But now, I had no credit. I'd gone through bankruptcy. I'd just spent five thousand dollars to get here. Could I really be so irresponsible? Well, no...I couldn't. So I left the little shop, joined our tour group and put the ring out of my mind—for about half an hour! Because suddenly, without warning, the ring flashed before my eyes a hundred times bigger than it was, the ruby blinding me, the silver and gold rings pulsating. Crazy, right? But even crazier was the message I got.

"Buy the ring. It is the Rose."

What? The Rose? Wait...I know this...yes...with a

small uprising of a new feeling I hadn't felt in a while…
what was that…it's familiar…it's…it's excitement. It's
a feeling of anticipation of something great about to
happen—and I felt touched by an angel. I could feel it in
every bone in my body and in that very second, I turned
to my friend and said I have to go buy that ring. Don't let
the bus leave without me.

And off I went, running like a madwoman through
the streets of a foreign country, looking for a tiny shop on
unfamiliar streets. I couldn't believe I found it. It was such
a little hole in the wall kind of place.

The sales woman was still there, saying in her broken
English that another woman had tried on the ring and
might come back as I did—a typical sales' move—but
before she could finish, I said, "I want it!" I put it on my
ring finger, and it looked like it belonged there, like it
had been there forever. In my mind, I had just made a
wedding vow to myself. To love, honor and cherish…till
death do *me* part!

Now you might be thinking that's the end of the
story. But it's not. We left Florence within an hour of my
purchase, and after driving through the Tuscany Valley, we
ended up in the walled city of Assisi. This was the ancient
city where St. Francis began his monastery. He is known as
one of the most Jesus-like saints. He was born into riches
and denounced them all when God asked him to build a
church for the poor. The story of his sainthood is beautifully
depicted in his Basilica. Something about this man touched
my soul. But I didn't know what it was until later.

As we entered the cathedral with the tour, the guide sat us in this beautiful chapel adorned with icons and azure blue domes. The minute I sat there, I felt such a profound sadness that my tears became uncontrollable. I cried with abandon, unashamedly, even as others watched and wondered what the hell was wrong with this woman. Even my friend couldn't get through the veil of sorrow I was in. The weird thing is it didn't feel like my own. My thoughts were not of my story, but the story of love gone...of joy that perished...of light gone out of the world. This was so huge I could barely contain it.

But the craziest thing was that the minute we left this chapel, the intense feelings went away instantly. Just gone. I had no residual thoughts, no explanation, just my tear streaked face and the tissue I was holding.

When the tour was over, we entered the little gift shop run by the Franciscan monks. Icons adorned the walls. Statues filled the shelves. I was drawn to a basket on the counter that had small medallions with St. Francis on one side. When I turned it over to see the other side, I almost dropped the medallion as I gasped. My friend heard me and came running.

"What's the matter?" she asked.

"Look, I said to her," and I held the medallion with one hand as I raised my hand on which my new wedding ring sat. It was unbelievable. The medallion had a red stone surrounded by a silver ring, which was surrounded by a gold ring. It was the same symbol. Wow!!!! I had no idea what it meant. But the words, "It is the rose" once again rang in my ears.

Hours later as we lay in our beds looking over the pamphlets with the history of Assisi, my friend came across a picture of the chapel we had visited that day. The one in which the sorrow of all sorrows overtook me. This time it was her turn to gasp!

"What is it," I asked.

"It was the chapel of Mary Magdalene," she said.

And I felt chills running all over my body. Mary Magdalene. The Rose. OMG! And in that instant I knew that there is a message here for me. St. Francis loved Mary Magdalene as the woman who was the first disciple to Jesus Christ, as the woman who saw Jesus at his ascension, and I believe, as the woman who loved him as he loved her. I believe that together they were the Ying and Yang, the Divine Masculine and the Divine Feminine incarnated to walk the planet together and teach us all the Way of Love...the Way of Mastery...the way of being both fully human and fully divine. This belief fills me with hope, with a sense of purpose, with a feeling that goes beyond my little ego and its sense of righteousness.

Mary Magdalene was named a prostitute and sinner by history, by a Pope and by the disciples who were jealous of her relationship with Jesus. She suffered the betrayal of those around her who misunderstood, who condemned, who led her teacher to his death. And still, she held on to her divinity and her ability to forgive the unforgivable. I knew in that instant that she is with me, helping me to move beyond the pain into the truth about love, into the understanding of purpose, into the possibility that something great will come from all I'm going through. She is the Rose.

And so Italy was not just about pizza. I didn't feed my body, but I did feed my soul. I think that's an important thing for me right now. It gives me a broader perspective, and maybe that's part of the journey. To get through this chaotic emotional time, I need to believe in something beyond myself, perhaps steering the ship a bit. I like that. Even if it's just pretend...it works for me right now.

INSIGHTS:

I know that you may not believe the same things I believe, but that doesn't mean that our beliefs can't help us in some way. A belief is one of two things. It may be unconscious, and we can only see the glimpse of it through our behaviors, i.e. "I believe I'm not good enough; therefore, I don't apply myself in areas in which I'm uncomfortable." We all know about those limiting beliefs.

Or it is the other kind of belief, those we choose, like a belief in God, the Law of Attraction, certain philosophies or suppositions. And these choices are always based on one thing. The belief makes us feel better. Better than what you might ask? Better than we feel without it.

The truth is no one can factually substantiate a belief. And in my opinion, they shouldn't have to. It's enough for me to know that you choose this belief because it gives you solace. It grounds you in times of stress. It provides you hope for something bigger. It allows you to gently sit with your pain knowing it "has come to pass." So whatever your belief at this time, I say go for it. Let it guide you, provide you with some peace, invite you to anticipate good times to come. For me, it is Mary Magdalene. She has been my guide for many years, and I had no idea why. Now her presence makes sense. She is teaching me something, or better said, she is reminding me of something I've forgotten. I still don't know what that is, but I feel better knowing someday…I will.

THROUGH THE FIRE

I wish I could say that my ex no longer has any hold on me. But unfortunately, he does. We still own a business together that I depend on for my finances and which he has total control over.

Even after I left him, moving to a new town to get away, he still continued to call, text and email me, telling me he loved me and missed me. And so I would ask, "Do you feel better when you say those words to me?" His answer was, "Yes, I do."

"But I don't," I told him.

Because if those words were true, why did you let me leave? Why didn't you champion our marriage? Why did you treat me like an enemy? Why?

And of course there is never an answer. He just wanted me to hang on to hope, telling me he's confused or fucked up, not wanting me to be completely gone from his life until he had another woman securely by his side. It made the grieving process difficult. Because although a huge part of me knew I was done and could never go back, a small part of me continued to hope—hope that he would change, hope that he really did love me. Meanwhile, my life was on hold. I was in a new town, a new home, making new friends, and yet still feeling tethered to an old life that was an illusion.

The game continued over months, and in those months, there was more rejection, more harassment, more disrespect. We would talk on the phone, text back and forth, even visited each other a few times. The cord between us so strong, he would pull me toward him with words and then push me aside with heinous actions that would leave me on the ground. Until one day after a very disturbing conversation that left me feeling rejected, I suddenly realized that it really wasn't him disrespecting me anymore. It was me!

I was the one allowing him to treat me as if I was unworthy of his love, despite the fact that it was he who had betrayed our marriage. In one swift moment, it was like I woke up. I didn't answer his calls or his texts. That continued for several months during which time I began to deal with my losses, grieve openly, and let go.

Two months later, I finally contacted him. Our anniversary was that week, and I was feeling strong enough to connect with him. We were still married after all. Looking back, I know I was testing my resolve—my strength, my personal power. We made a date to spend the weekend with each other. I was committed to being completely present, not having sex, and really feeling what it was like for me to be in his presence.

What I found was that I felt empowered for the first

time in a long while within the relationship. In those two days, I saw how every conversation was started by me and was about him. He never asked what I was doing with my life or how the kids were or the family. I saw how the relationship had been one-sided for a very long time. We had no common interests, common values, or common dreams.

During those two days together, after months of no contact, he used pity to try to manipulate my feelings. He talked about how lonely he was, how he couldn't forgive himself for what he'd done—all in the effort of making me feel sorry for him in a play for control. All I felt in those moments was compassion. I had done some of my grieving, and I had let go to some degree. I no longer wanted or expected anything from him. I could finally look at him, be with him, talk with him—without hurting, without longing, without needing his love to feel validated and complete. And I thought perhaps we could be friends—that our eighteen years together didn't all have to become a lie.

I told him then I loved him and always would. At the time, I thought that was true. Maybe it is. I'm not sure. I think I loved the man I thought he was, certainly not the stranger he turned out to be. I realized that my loving him was not about his worthiness of my love, rather about my capacity for love. And I felt peaceful.

Still, there was no talk of divorce. Why? Because we owned a business together and he was afraid that he wouldn't be able to buy me out, so he continued to "court" me, if you can call it that. He was once again nice and tender one moment, rejecting and cruel the next. Just two weeks later, I sensed that he had been with someone else while he was still telling me he loved me. I'm not sure how I knew, but I've had many intuitive moments and have learned to listen to that very tiny, quiet voice. He denied it of course. But when three weeks went by and he refused to talk to me, even about business matters, I knew that he'd already found his next conquest. Pictures on Facebook confirmed it, so I was finally ready to put an end to it all.

I decided to get divorced. And I made it easy: no lawyers, no fight, just a signature on the dotted line. You keep your IRA; I keep mine—and we'd both remain partners in the business. That was the easiest and fastest way to end the marriage. There'd be no alimony or attorneys. Seventeen years of marriage...filed, stamped, and dissolved by a judge's signature in five days.

It would be over, right? No more games. No more lies. No more insults. No more control or manipulation. Now we would just be business partners, putting the past behind us. I ask if we can be business partners and friends: be respectful, be kind, and work together to make the business profitable enough to sell some day. Even after all I'd learned about him and all I'd been through, I still wanted to believe that somehow we could work together and wipe out all the bad stuff with a divorce decree. Naive again, I know. What was his answer to my question?

"I have two job offers in the valley," he said.

"Hmm, great. Does that mean you want to sell," I ask?

"I'm working 70 hours a week here, and I can't leave. It's my baby," he said.

"Ok. So sounds like you're tired. You have another job offer, and I'm still not sure if you are answering my questions about us being able to work together as partners and friends," I said once more, as I recognized the familiar pattern to our longtime conversations in which he never really answers the question, instead saying things to distract me, take me down another avenue that leads to some dead end where I'm cornered.

"I don't want to give you hope," he said. OMG, is he crazy? I'm the one who asked for the divorce while he swore there was no one else and wasn't sure he was ready to give up on our marriage. That is how he always twisted things so that I couldn't tell what was up or what was down. None of his words were making sense, and I could feel him playing me. That odd familiar sensation that I'm about to go down the rabbit hole again was niggling at my heart. But I knew what's down there—NOTHING! At the bottom was nothing but desperation, hopelessness, powerlessness and pain.

My mind spun; the words became jumbled, as the fear escalated in every fiber of my being. In my confusion, he reached out to me, took me in his arms, and I felt something new crawling, creeping just under my awareness. It scared me. My mind and heart wanted to shut out the truth and pretend he cared, that he wasn't a liar, that I could trust him—again—even after all the lies! But part of me was thinking, "What's wrong with you, girl?"

He continued with words of comfort, and as I once again softened to his touch, becoming his prey, he knew I was caught in the trap. His words became caustic, blaming, as he justified his actions by telling me he's a nice guy.

A nice guy! I heard that from the long dark tunnel I'd just descended into. He's told me that for years. But do nice guys have to tell you that they are nice guys all the time? The question rolled around in my head, and all of a sudden I was no longer in the tunnel. The light was bright and that creeping feeling was now full blown. It was big... powerful. It was something raw and savage.

ANGER!

Anger at him. Anger at her. Anger at how my life had turned out. Anger at all I'd lost and all he'd taken. My anger was dark, rich, full-bodied. It was alive and breathing, seething with words so long held back, with truths unspoken for fear of abandonment. This anger, like fire, burned away the cobwebs of confusion, of denial, and I saw things clearly for the first time in years.

I was abandoned. I was unloved.

And it was not just today, not just when he had an affair, NO! He'd abandoned me years ago when he rejected me as punishment for not giving in to his selfish demands. He abandoned me when he undermined every attempt I made at creating a successful career. He abandoned me every time some challenge showed up or some situation needed to be handled in our lives, forcing me to deal with the crisis alone—telling me I was better equipped than he to take care of it all. He never acknowledged the value of what I'd accomplished if it worked out as he wanted, but blamed me every time if it didn't. He abandoned me every time he told lies about me to others just to make himself look good. The truth is he was never really there. He had lied to me from the very beginning of the relationship. But I was too trusting, and he was just that good a liar.

These memories flashed through me as the anger built, and for the first time in probably 17 years, I WAS BACK! I no longer felt hopelessness or despair. I no longer yearned for something I was now clear I never had. I no longer was willing to consider that any of his words were valid. In one fell swoop, I moved from the depths of the darkness where death felt like the only answer to the heights of my power...

And like Scarlet O'Hara, I stood, fist in the air, and said, "As God is my witness I will never allow you to hurt me, manipulate me or abuse me again!"

I let him have it, all of it. I stood there raging for the first time since I found out he was having an affair because for the first time I didn't care at all about his feelings. I didn't care if I'd ever see him again, didn't care if he "still liked me." Oh my God! I couldn't believe the years of anger I had pent up—the things that I never said, that I kept hidden because the saying of them might have ended my marriage a long time ago.

I screamed, yelled, went down the litany of things

he'd done to me, the lies he'd told me, the cruelty he inflicted on me. Everything...everything came out like bile so long held in me that I hadn't even recognized the impact of that pain in my body until I released it.

Oh, it felt good. And I thought I'd gotten it all out, but it was only the start.

One week later, he announced on Facebook that he was in a relationship and in love. Everyone commented on how happy they were for him, how *they* belonged together; I felt sick.

Once again he betrayed me from a distance. He'd told me only two weeks earlier that he didn't want the divorce, that he still loved me...and it took everything I had to stay neutral and follow through with the divorce. But there was still, and I say this begrudgingly, some part of me that wanted to believe him even after all the lies.

I was angry, angry...angry! Only this time, I wasn't sharing my anger with him. No. He knew how I felt about him now. Instead, I shared this anger with my family and friends, but they said let it go. Move on. You don't want him. He's a horrible man. All true. Then they said your anger will make you sick. Oh, crap, I thought, that's just what I needed—to get some horrible disease on top of everything else! So I listened; I breathed. I let the dragon go back to sleep...

But in doing so, I lost sight of myself again. I fell back into that abyss of darkness, and the cycle started all over again. I wondered when it would all stop. What did I have to do to get off of this merry-go-round? Instead of anger, I was once again feeling depressed.

You get it, right? You know what I'm talking about? It's like being stuck on a treadmill that has two speeds, fast and faster, and there's no "off" button.

As I sit here writing this, so many other memories flood me. I vacillate between emotions that hurt my heart. It's not just about him. I realize my reality is constantly reflecting powerlessness and anger. I keep having experiences that keep me feeling stuck in the injustice that has become my life.

Can you relate? It's things like an email getting lost that changes an outcome I expect to be good into something that hurts me financially, or on a wonderful trip to Italy, I first get eaten alive by an Italian spider, leaving welts the size of golf balls all over my body and then fall on two thousand year old bricks and scrape my knee like a little girl. Then, I buy a beautiful ring to honor my now empty wedding finger and lose the ruby within two days. I mean really, come on God...give me a break!

And what do you think happens? My "break" comes: an heirloom, antique brandy set, Venetian glass with silver inlay, sitting on a credenza in my living room suddenly is broken, hit by a falling decorative tile he and I bought in Mexico on our honeymoon. Talk about irony!!! Something I cherished was shattered by something had I loved.

The message? Come on, it's not that obscure. In fact, it was so clear to me in that instant that I fell to my knees and wept, wept for the woman I once was and wept for the woman I had become.

I had let something I cherished, and more importantly

believed I needed—him, my marriage, my home, my financial security—destroy something I should have loved more. Me!

In that moment, I knew I could not change anything. Not the emails, not the spiders, not the falling debris of my life, and certainly not him. I didn't have the power to fix the world, make others do the right thing, control what they say or what they think. My anger and despair wasn't affecting their lives, only mine.

I had been broken, or at least cracked, when the illusion of the life I was living was torn open, and the scars ran deep. I sat with that thought for a few days. I prayed and meditated. I asked for guidance—a sign—something to help me see, through my tears, the real woman behind the curtain.

In the midst of despair the phone rang and my coach, an amazing intuitive woman, was calling. I was weeping, but I answered. Immediately, she knew she had called at the right time. She asked the questions that illicit answers of which even the unsaid words can be heard. From somewhere deep inside this insightful woman came the question that no one dares ask for fear of what it might bring out in me. But she wasn't afraid.

"What has he done now?" she said with frustration in her voice.

And the dam in me broke; the words began tumbling out, one after the other. The anger building once more...

I heard her say, "That Fucker! I swear I am ready to go after him with you!"

And it didn't stop there. She went on and on, practically screaming herself, saying all the things he'd done to me, the things I'd shared with her over the past few months. She spewed so many angry, righteous words about him—even going as far as to say she'd come help me beat him up along with her six brothers—that I began to chuckle. The fire inside me finally, finally began to burn out, to lose its heat, and I was left with the embers slowly dying. Some part of me was feeling heard, relieved, awakened. Some part of me recognized how she'd given me the space to feel my rage.

And as I did, something shifted again. At first, it was very slight, like a feather tickling my nose. Then, it slowly grew: down my spine, into my belly, through my feet and deep into the earth. If I had to give this sensation a color, it would be green—fresh, new, like the first bud of spring. I noticed the prickly sensation I'd been feeling for years begin to dissipate and in its place was a gentle flow of ease. Just that. Ease. Relief perhaps is also a good word, relief from the pain of helplessness and the fire of rage that had no place to go, no action it could take but to burn itself out. And in the ashes, I found me!

As I write this, I'm reminded of a dream I had when I was 18 years old. I was standing on a huge boulder at the foot of a cliff, the ocean spray covering me with each wave. I stood there in white, my hair flowing in the wind. Suddenly, there was a burst of fire from the stone beneath my feet, and I became...the phoenix.

It was a powerful dream even then. But now as I

remember it, the meaning becomes so much clearer. Out of the fire, I am transformed. I still don't have all the answers, but I do know that I'm done telling this old story, that I am more than this story that I have let define me for too long. If I had to blame anyone, unfortunately, it would be me now. I'm the one keeping me stuck.

Trust me when I say, I know how hard it is to accept that. Because the reality is things were done to us, in some way, shape or form—things that hurt, things that changed us temporarily into someone we didn't recognize. But today? Today we are responsible for two things, the only two things we can ever truly control, change, or fix.

Those two things are our thoughts and our responses. I've known this and taught this, but hell, I am now ready to embrace it. Because once the despair and anger were released, I could see that tiny glimmer of that small white candle burning in the window of my soul, lighting the way back home. I can't say exactly what that feeling is except the absence of the feelings I'd been swimming in for over a year. Some might say I was numb, and perhaps that is true. But whatever it is, it is better. Perhaps it is only a brief reprieve, or perhaps it is the opening of a door into something new. That is what I choose to believe. I'm determined to go through that door.

INSIGHTS:

Depression is something too many of us know about. From the moment of diagnosis, we rush to conquer it with pills, yoga and meditation. I wonder. I wonder if depression isn't simply the result of deeply suppressing righteous anger. I think about the well-meaning anger management classes that grew in popularity in the early 70's and see a correlating climb in depression (to epic proportions) since their inception. I think of those clients, friends, and even family members who suffer from depression and try to remember when or if I've ever heard them be angry? Why are we so afraid of anger?

Certainly acting on our anger in a fit of passion, rage, revenge, etc. is unacceptable. But suppressing anger is just as harmful in the end. What we need to do is learn how to express this rich, fiery emotion in a healthy way. Because if we don't, I'm afraid we will not heal. The energy it takes to suppress anger is so big, so overwhelming, that it requires us to numb ourselves down. Depression isn't sadness...it's nothingness. It's living without feeling anything. Life is dull. Nothing keeps our attention. We can't focus. There is no meaning, and therefore, we don't act. And life passes us by while we are disengaged, sometimes causing havoc, which results in our feeling great amounts of only one other feeling—anxiety. Oh, what a screwed-up cycle! And I find myself in it.

And Time Inches By

Just the other day, I got a certified letter from him offering to buy me out of our business. It was something he had an opportunity to do when I first left and again when I asked for a divorce. He didn't do it then though, and I thought that was a good thing for me. I would continue to get a salary while I took the time to heal and to reinvent myself. I thought, rather naively again, that we could work on improving the value of this business together. At least, that's what he said back then.

Now it is another lie to add to the list. Only this time, I feel responsible because by now I should have known better. The problem is that the offer was lower than my initial investment. I know now from all I'd learned about him in this last year, that this offer was only a first step. But a first step to what? A negotiation? Or a way to force me out?

While he had agreed that we would run this business as partners to accomplish this "easy" divorce, it became evident that as I was stepping back into a business we both owned, he still and always would consider it his own. In the weeks that followed our divorce, I had requested a copy of the books. This infuriated him, and later I would find out that he had told the employees I was unhappy with them, that I believed they were spending too much of our money, and that I hated the business. He began an email campaign threatening to cut me off if I didn't sell the business to him. I tried to stay professional and not react. I tried to let go of the past hurts and work with him as a partner. I begged him to remember that we had spent 18 years together and not to make our whole life a lie—all in vain. No matter how many times I released the story of his lying and cheating, felt the grief so that I could forgive him too, he continued to treat me as an enemy, reminding me over and over again that he was not the man I once thought he was.

My fear reared up again like a snake uncoiling. And on the day I received that certified letter, I could feel the venom in his offer and sense that the strike would come next week when he would suddenly decide not to send me my salary. But before it could paralyze me, I decided to see an attorney. I have to pat myself on the back for finally recognizing that contact with him was caustic to me and that I needed someone to stand up for me. I had to protect myself from all the fearful feelings he instigated in me. If I didn't have my own power yet, then letting someone act on my behalf was as close as I could get to safety for now.

The attorney told me what my legal rights were and helped me to see that I lawfully was entitled to half the company's worth. She sent him a letter with a counter offer and established within this offer the parameters of legal actions we would take if he unlawfully decided not to pay me. I walked out of her office feeling empowered. I felt for the first time that someone was not only validating me and acknowledging my feelings but was also ready to go to bat for me. Even though I knew I was paying her to do so, it still felt great!

A week later, he did as predicted. He didn't pay me. And once again I felt the fear, the worry of how I would pay my bills without that money? I tried with all my might to squelch those fears, to find my power again, but it was really hard. Fear is such a huge emotion, and the mind runs away with it like a bullet train zipping by all the things that could go wrong. I know you know that feeling!

My friend came to the rescue and reminded me that no matter what he tried to do, I was still an owner of the business with rights that he couldn't take away. I just had to focus my attention on that and step into a place of trust: trusting my attorney to take the next step, trusting myself not to fall to pieces, trusting the Universe-God-Source as the benevolent energy it is. It was hard, given how much I'd lost in the last few years—a husband, a friend, a home, a community. It seemed hard to continue to have faith that something bigger and better was coming toward me—if I could only hold on to that belief that out of every adversity comes something great.

My attorney did take care of it. I won't bore you with the details of how, but I will say I was paid my salary within two hours of some strategic calls. Once again, I felt relief. But more importantly, I realized: that life can quickly turn on a dime and then flip again; that it was sometimes within my control and most times not; that I had nothing but trust available to me and that was much more powerful than fear; and that even if I hadn't been paid, there was a huge part of me that finally knew that there was nothing he could do to hurt me again because I wasn't alone. I had resources. I'd be okay no matter what.

So, he did creep back into my life and my head for two days. And I kicked him out quicker than a bad tenant. I practiced the feeling of what my life would look like once I was bought out of the company, how I could create a new business of my own, put money into my current business, and create the financial security I once had on my own. In doing so, I could feel my worry and my fear slowly subside.

Instead, I feel a new feeling. I began to notice that although I could push aside thoughts of him for long periods of time, I was still feeling disappointment in myself for making him the center of my world to the exclusion of my own needs. I look around at my reality and ask myself, "What's next?" How do I begin to create the life I want? I realize the more I am taking action in my daily routine that moves me toward a goal, the less I think of him. And that's a good thing. I know I'm not in his head, and I'm frustrated that I've given him so much space in mine. So I dust myself off, turn my thoughts to other things, and deal with my despondency.

I have always been a planner, able to look ahead and see my next dream so clearly that my enthusiasm was infectious. But where did that me go? Instead of excitement, I feel overwhelmed. There are so many directions I could start out on, yet none of them feel compelling. After everything I've been through, I want something good to happen. I yearn for an opportunity to show up that will excite me, ignite my passion, direct my next step, and move me beyond where I am now. I am so tired of waiting: waiting for these feelings to go away, waiting for the understanding of why this all happened, waiting to feel ready for a new relationship.

A part of me is skeptical. I look back and think if I could be in denial about the life I was living for so long, about how unhappy I was, about how little I listened to my intuition and put aside my own desires, how would I ever know what is true? How would I ever be able to have the life I want? I try to think positively, but then something happens, and I feel that nothing will ever change. I fear that this is my life now—alone, sometimes scared, and sometimes frustrated. You know what I'm talking about, don't you? It's like waiting for the phone call to come from someone who is offering you a free ticket to see your favorite rock band perform. You know it's possible. You've placed the raffle ticket into the bucket. You could win it just as easily as someone else. So why not you? But then, you remember you never have won anything. You've always had to work hard to get what you wanted. Nothing was ever handed to you for free. You sweep that thought from your mind and vacillate back and forth from "Do I wait for the free ticket?" to "Do I make this happen and go buy one?"

That's where I'm at. Do I wait for some sign as to what I should be doing next to move my life toward an unknown dream, or do I go get a job and resign myself to this life—a life without magic, love, surprises, or passion? I think about this a lot. I have been an entrepreneur for over 30 years, creating my own businesses and passionately making a difference in the lives of others. But here I was feeling depleted with nothing to give, too wounded to offer solace to others, too confused about who I am to know what I can do, too untrusting of myself to venture out into the big bad world.

I've met so many women in the last two years who are living in this space after their experience with an abusive relationship. Coming out of that relationship after years of emotional and mental abuse leaves one vacillating between anxiety and paralysis, between disappointment and overwhelm. They wonder how they will ever recognize and trust love again, not trusting themselves or their judgement, let alone the hidden motives of others.

I get it. I've felt it. But I don't want my life to be defined by what others have done to me. I want to be the designer of my own experience. I want to find the gem in it, the thing that helps me become more: more of who I am and more of who I came to be. I want to reclaim my joy, my passion, myself. And I wonder what that would look like.

As these thoughts run through my head, I feel my pessimism gnawing at me. All those who love me are constantly telling me I need to take care of myself, that it is time I loved me as much as I had loved him. It surprises me how much those comments bother me because "loving oneself" is a pretty typical thing a counselor helps others do for themselves. Yet, like most people, I didn't know what that actually meant.

What did it look, sound, and feel like to truly love myself? So many times as I'd told my clients that it was important for them to love themselves, they'd agree and then ask, "How do I do that?" We can so easily see what "not" loving ourselves looks like and sounds like. We know when we are self-critical, self-deprecating, and denying our truth that we are not being kind to ourselves, let alone loving ourselves.

But when asked what does it mean to be loving to yourself, most people will say things like: I treat myself to something nice; I give myself space; I take a nap when I'm tired; I read a good book; I go to counseling; I stop saying mean things to myself; I exercise and take care of my body, etc.

And all those things are good. But what I found as I tried to do all those things was that I wasn't feeling the LOVE! I was going through the motions for sure. But there were definitely no warm fuzzies. I just couldn't find a way of loving myself that made me feel better.

When I reflect back on it all, the one thing that really showed up was that, despite my healthy self-esteem and self-worth, I didn't really know how to love myself. Even after all that I've learned about human nature—all the skill I had in counseling, all the intuition I experienced about people—I didn't know a thing about self-love.

I want more than anything to know what self-love feels like, sounds like, looks like in a physical way—something tangible, something identifiable—because I know that is the only way I could be sure that I was loving me, rather than just puffing up my feathers, putting on a smile, and saying, "yes, I'm great" when I really wasn't. You know what I'm talking about.

So I went on a journey through my life. I started reading my journals. I talked with my family about "who I really am," asking them to tell me about what they saw in me. I read books, did exercises, went to counseling and participated in programs that promised to heal my broken heart and help me find my purpose.

But despite all the good advice, what I finally discovered was something no one had ever told me, something I'd never thought of before. (And I think of things all the time!) It was something that actually helped me to understand what loving myself really meant, and the amazing thing is that once I got it, everything else really became easier: things like gratitude, faith and hope. Pretty cool, huh?

Now, let me be clear. This thing called "loving yourself" is something you must practice and play with because it is most likely not something you have ever really felt or understood as "loving yourself."

It's not something that you give to yourself. It's not some big action. It's not even just changing your thoughts. It's a feeling so HUGE and so simple that when you experience it, you'll know. Loving yourself is a choice. It occurs in the little things, the small moments of life experiences.

That is a big realization for me, and one that I am playing with. The first thing that I looked at was how I love others. What is it that I offer them, which is so valuable to me that in offering it I am saying to them how much I love them and how important they are to me? Big question! Big answer!

Here's what I discovered. Deep inside me, I have core values that drive my thoughts, my actions, and my behaviors. Those values are so integrated with who I am that identifying them was not easy. I'm not sure how they come about or if they are the same for everyone. I suspect they are not, which explains why different people express love differently.

I've recognized what my core values are by allowing myself to stay with the hurt feeling I experience when I'm not receiving that value from another. It's easy to simply blame someone else for not loving us or to say to ourselves that our expectations are too high. That's when we get angry, right? We feel misunderstood, rejected, and confused by another's behavior. I know you've been there just like I have. But staying there with that judgement, either about them or about our worthiness, stunts our expansion and shuts off the knowledge of what love is to us.

When I stayed with the feeling of hurt—without judgement—I realized that what I'd wanted, what I'd expected from another, was the very important thing that I give when I love them. Wow! It's so simple, isn't it? Yet like me, I'm sure that you have never truly understood this about yourself.

One of my big core values is loyalty. Oh yes, I have changed careers, started all kinds of businesses, and had many different passions, but the one thing that has always been true is that I am absolutely loyal to people. That loyalty shows up not only in my support of them when they are at their best but also when they are at their worst.

I don't give up on them, even if they've given up on themselves. I may not like their behavior, but I understand the wound that drives it; therefore, I am compassionate and give them slack. I stand up for them and defend them even when I know they are wrong by helping others to have compassion. My empathy runs deep for them when they are hurting. All these actions on my part come from my sense of loyalty. As Martha Stewart would say, "It's a good thing."

...except when I am so loyal to another that I am absolutely disloyal to myself. If I allow someone to whom I am loyal to be disloyal to me, then I am not loving myself. Profound, right?

And this is true with all my core values. Honesty is also one of them. And when I let another be dishonest with me, either by choosing to trust them more than I trust myself or making excuses for their lies, then I am being dishonest to myself—again, not loving myself.

Relationships matter to me. I have always said that I cannot truly know myself without relationships. That's how I know that I'm funny, compassionate, wise, etc., by experiencing myself expressing those values in a relationship. So when I allow someone to treat me like I don't matter—to discount my needs, thoughts, or feelings—then I am discounting myself. I am not loving me enough to know my worth. This is so simple, and yet so hard sometimes, right? Your values may be completely different than mine. But whatever they are, they are important enough to you that it is from that value that you love someone else. And it is when you ignore that value in yourself that you are not loving you.

I remember one day before my divorce when I was planning to go to my home town to spend some time with him. This was at a time when I still hoped that something would change. He was going away for the weekend with his son. I knew he needed the time off, and I was fine with that. Loyal to his needs! Respecting his desires! But when I asked him in a text when we could go away together and he brushed me aside, telling me "someday" and we'd talk about it later that night—but only after he watched the basketball game—something inside me shifted.

In that moment, I felt so undervalued, so disrespected, in other words, very unloved. As I picked up my phone to answer his text, getting ready to say, "Sure, that's fine," an inner voice said: "Really? He's made it clear you are not important, and you are saying the same thing." That's when I realized that although I was hurt by his words and actions, I was even more hurt by my own. If I responded as I usually did, then it was me that was disrespecting and undervaluing myself, not him! So I didn't answer. And you know what?

It felt great. It felt empowering. It felt good to know I respected myself enough to act on my behalf in a loving way. There were no angry words to him, no recriminations or whining, and no explanation of how I felt because none of that mattered. The only thing that mattered was that I was finally loving myself by respecting myself despite his lack of respect for me.

I hope that my resolve and understanding of this way of loving myself will become easy to sustain. Because I also know in loving "me," I let go of my fear. Fear cannot exist in the same place that love dwells. Fear is simply a feeling of not being safe, and safety is one of our hard wired imperatives. We all know that. We understand that the ego's job is to "find the answers," "be aware of dangers," and "protect us at all costs." There is nothing more unsafe than feeling unloved. But we cannot always look for love from others to make us safe because sometimes they are just not capable of loving us, or sometimes they can't love us enough.

INSIGHTS:

I believe that understanding how you love another and knowing what values you offer them will help you to know how to truly love yourself. There is such a sense of peace and empowerment when you discover what love is to you. Not only because you can now act in accordance with that kind of loving towards yourself, but also because you now know what you are really asking for from another. Hmmm. That makes so much sense to me. It makes it something I can easily speak about. Perhaps if I'd known this years ago, I might have trusted the information I was getting and not gone through what I've been through. But then as the caterpillar that I had been, there would have been something else I'd have fed on in order to grow. Perhaps the only way for me to learn these things was to enter the cocoon. It is a lonely place at times, at other times a scary place. You are living within your own conscious and unconscious. If you allow it—stay present with it—insights come. Something new awakens in you. Hmmm. I think I'm becoming more comfortable in the void.

Out of Doubt Comes a Kind of Clarity

I sit here on this rainy Oregon day—fire glowing, lights dim, my cat curled at my feet—and I realize that my thoughts no longer provoke anger. Somehow, I have come to accept the changes in my life. My home—comfy and cozy, filled with the things I love—is my haven, my very own space. I have built altars in every room so that I am reminded always that the divine is with me. And I wait for guidance, a direction...some sign that will show me what I need to do next.

Have you ever done that? Prayed for miracles? Searched for meaning? Sat in the silence listening for that still inner voice that will tell you who you are and what you are becoming, only to be faced with words that you doubt, even as the voice tells you how loved you are?

How loved I am? Really? Why can't I feel that?

As the smoke clears from the ashes that have become my life, I look around me and feel disappointed, even as I feel appreciation for my new home, my new friends, my new freedom to choose for myself my next experience.

My mind is exhausted from all the self-analysis, my heart vulnerable in the quiet that surrounds me. My body fluctuates between the need to sleep and rejuvenate and the need to move, keep moving, and keep going no matter what.

It's really not about regrets, even for those losses, decisions or outcomes that were unexpected. I've always been kind of a risk taker, impulsively jumping into new adventures, willing to lose because I was not willing to stop dreaming big.

I look back on my life, and I can see the things I accomplished, those things that matter most: raising four beautiful, honest, authentic children who have blessed my life in so many ways; the work I did with clients, helping them to reach beyond their limitations, their patterned and conditioned beliefs, into the life they were destined to live; and helping the aging live their last days with dignity, expressing their wisdom, helping us to see that in the end nothing matters but love.

Oh yes, I feel proud of those moments where I touched the lives of others, and they so profoundly touched mine. I remember other things too like singing on stage to thousands, writing two books, acting in plays, scoring 200 in bowling, decorating my homes with love, even raising pigs and other farm animals like a real country girl from New York City.

I'm sure if you sat down and thought about it, you too, would remember things you've done, things that felt good in the doing. You'd come up with a list of decisions you were proud of, actions that took you to emotional highs you hadn't expected. Just remembering makes you feel better, doesn't it?

But that feel better feeling is hard to maintain when the lights are low, and you are by yourself. Your mind is a machine after all—its job to keep thinking, to look for answers to questions both conscious and unconscious, to keep you safe by reminding you of the things that didn't go so well so that you can refrain from making the same mistakes.

And that's when the worry and disappointment come knocking on your mind's door. I've felt disappointment with others for sure, but mostly disappointment in myself. Now that the anger has been defused, what's left are the "if onlys" and the "what ifs."

No matter what has happened, these thoughts come like ghosts in the night, making me wonder what would be different today had I done something different, had I known what I know now, had I said the right thing.

And the wondering continues...

Those thoughts lead me down to a place where I question myself to no end. Where I say things to myself like: "You were so dumb"; "You were so blind"; "You were so co-dependent!" Oh that's a great one.

Then, I look at myself in the mirror and see an old woman looking back—eyes sagging, wrinkles more pronounced, hair graying at the temples—and I worry about who will love me now?

Will I ever find love? Will I ever be able to trust

again? And I'm not just saying trust another person. I'm wondering if I can trust myself, my judgement and my desires. Will they take me to another heartache? Will I ever find my passion again?

But here's the astonishing thing! As all these thoughts run rampant in my mind, I realize that for the first time in a long time, I'm not thinking about him! I've moved to a place where my thoughts are about me. Me! And yes, sometimes they are negative. They are recriminating. They are kind of mean. But I find myself feeling good about it somehow, finding my mind no longer consumed by "his" life, but instead by my own.

I feel good, maybe even a little surprised.

Has that ever happened to you? Is it the mind's way of protecting itself from overload? I don't know for sure, but I like that feeling of realizing that hours, sometimes a few days, have gone by without my slipping back into the story that hurts.

It reminds me of a time when I had a dislocated tailbone and was in chronic pain. I had spent three years going from one doctor to another, one practitioner to another, praying for relief and finding it nowhere. Then one day, I just said to myself, "Enough!" I would stop focusing on the pain and instead focus on the seconds and minutes when the pain was not there. At first, it only happened a few times a day, and during those times, I'd stop and relish the feeling of being pain-free, letting my body memorize that feeling again. Over time, those moments became hours, then days. Then one day, I realized the pain was gone.

I will occasionally feel it when I've been sitting on my ass too long, and that's a reminder for me to move, to take action, to do something different. So of course, there are still times when he creeps back in my mind. When all of a sudden, I'm wondering once more how all this happened. And I slowly pull myself out of these thoughts by acknowledging the feeling and taking some kind of action. I don't believe this is denial. I know what I feel. But I also know that the thoughts I'm thinking will not make the past situation change. They'll only make my present situation worse. I get that now.

Okay, so I've come a long way baby. At least that's what all my family and friends say. I have always been one to delve deep and furious, and once I get a hold of something, I do all I can to understand. But there are just some things that are not understandable. I'll really never be able to figure out how and why he could do the things he did, and still does, to me. It's a waste of my time and energy to ponder questions that will never be answered.

Still I ask! Bummer, right? I wonder if everything that happened was predestined or divinely-guided. Was it all a lesson or karmic debt? Am I really who I think I am—a healthy, level headed, intelligent woman? If so, then how could I let myself be so taken by this guy? Was I unconscious myself of my inner child when I fell in love with him? And if so, how will I know that I'm not doing the same thing next time?

Oh, I can drive myself a bit crazy with all these thoughts. One thing that came out of the haze of questions was a clear memory of the ending of my first marriage and the understanding I had of myself at that time.

I was 20 years old, a college student and sorority pledge when I met my first husband. He was president of his fraternity and admired by many. He had sweet, kind brown eyes and a broad smile. His demeanor was gentle, unassuming, and he was brilliant without arrogance.

After having had several relationships prior to meeting him with a bunch of "bad boys," young men who broke my heart, I had prayed fervently one night to God to bring me "the one" because I was no longer going to pick a guy for myself. I was surrendering that job to the big guy upstairs. I knew he had better judgement than I did.

One day, on the way to school, I heard a voice from the empty back seat of my car, declaring "Today is the day!" I know you are probably thinking I'm making this up, or I'm schizophrenic. I assure you neither is true. I heard this voice, loud and clear, and when I got to school—in the cafeteria, across a sea of students—I saw him standing there with my sorority sisters. We made eye contact. I came over to him. We talked briefly, and he walked me to class. Then he went back to my sisters and told them he was going to marry me someday. The rest, as they say, is history.

We were married two years later, and spent 18 years together. We had four beautiful children, bought, renovated, and sold eight homes. We went through hard times and fun times. We were really good friends. We didn't fight much, which was good, but we also didn't have very much to say to each other. At first, I thought it was because he was so easy-going. Later, I realized that his "laidback" demeanor was his way of operating in the world—avoiding conflict and real intimacy. But my need to be safe outweighed my desire for intimacy, and I know now that I had chosen this sweet man because, on an unconscious level, I knew he would never demand more from me than I could give. He would never manipulate me or intentionally hurt me in order to feel powerful. He would not control me, and in fact, he would give me the freedom to be, do, and have whatever I was capable of, without question.

That relationship worked well for a while, until I began to feel the weight of the responsibility I had in our relationship. I made all the big decisions, dealt with all the difficult situations, and planned all our "next steps." Our dance worked for us because he didn't want conflict or the responsibility that comes from making decisions for others, and I needed safety, which I could more easily assure if I was in control.

Why did I need safety? Control? Well, I needed it because my father was a sociopath/narcissist and a very abusive man. He was intelligent, ambitious, and charming. He was also a liar, a cheat, and a bully. I did what so many women do. The first time around I picked a man who was the complete opposite of my dad, and I am eternally grateful for that unconscious decision. This man, although emotionally detached, was a far better father and husband than my dad was. In fact, the safety I experienced in this marriage was exactly what I needed to explore deeper issues I didn't even know I had until after my father's death when I was 33 years old.

Soon after his death, as happens with many molested children, I began to have flashback memories I could not control or escape. I went through a year of therapy to heal that little girl within me who was hurting so badly that she did the only thing a little girl can do. She hid. She hid from me, and she hid in a relationship with a passionless, safe man. The sad part is when I finally found my own safety and no longer needed it from my husband, he couldn't step into the new role I was asking him to take. He couldn't take the responsibility I was now willing to relinquish or the control I was open to letting go of. Bottom line was I had changed, but he couldn't, at least not at that time or with me.

So our marriage ended gently, and we continued to parent our children in respectful and loving ways, continuing to participate as parents jointly in their lives. That is something I'm proud of. I had come to understand that my childhood experience had become my internal story driving the behaviors that made me look for this man of safety. I needed this experience with him to heal that two year old and let her know that not only is she safe but she didn't deserve what had happened to her. And when that marriage ended, though it was very sad, it was not devastating or destructive. I will forever be grateful to this man who helped me heal such a profound wound.

I had done a lot of emotional work and a lot of healing during that time. I stepped out into the world with a new feeling of strength, of openness, of vulnerability. I hoped and prayed for a new relationship. One filled with passion, emotion, excitement. And I got it. Right? Wrong!!!!!

What I didn't know, and have only now realized as I've been writing this book and living in the cocoon, was that just as my inner two year old had hand-picked my first husband to maintain a sense of safety, and in doing so, had found a man who was the complete opposite of my dad, there was still a 15 year old rebellious girl inside me who stepped forward from my unconscious and dared to pick a man who matched her father exactly. The same girl who had been picking those bad boys trying to make them love her the way her father never had, now stepped out of my unconscious to once again try to get what she needed from her father with a new bully of her own.

Boy was that a revelation, one that truly had me by the throat. I am unable even to speak of the level of disappointment I had for myself. How had I not known? How could I do something so typical of an incest survivor and be so unconscious for so many years? And how was I going to heal that girl who's need to be loved was so great she put herself in danger all the time—high risk behavior indeed. I feel so ashamed.

So you see, I could certainly identify and blame my second husband for the horrible things he did to me and continues to do to me today. But I have come face-to-face with the part of me now who is responsible for choosing him. And although I'd like to blame her, I know that does no good. I know that the healing of that young girl inside is my responsibility only. I have to be present to her need for love, her need of approval from men, her need to be seen and appreciated. I need her because while she carries the pain of abandonment, she also carries my passion and vibrance for life. I need her as much as she needs me. I just can't let her make all the decisions, especially those that are more appropriately handled by the mature adult me.

As that younger part, whose great need combined with her great naiveté, revealed her feelings to me, I felt compassion for her. In doing so, I am feeling more settled. The questions are subsiding a bit. The agony of doubt about my future feels less paralyzing. Pretty peculiar what happens when you spend time looking within at yourself, rather than outside at "him." You get a sense, perhaps only a slight one, but one nonetheless, that another shift is occurring. Another light has come on in that darkened tunnel, and your path starts to slowly materialize in front of you. You begin to think to yourself....hmmm...maybe just maybe...

I'm going to be okay... we're going to be okay...

INSIGHTS:

One of the ways to start that exploration is to first make a list of all that you have accomplished, achieved, and are proud of. Go as far back as you can, even to your childhood. It's important to start to see that there are great things about yourself. Our mind is so acutely aware of all the mistakes we've made. And that's good as far as keeping ourselves safe and doing better next time. Our mind is not so good about sharing all that is great about us. Although it makes us feel better, it doesn't really serve a purpose as far as the mind goes. But it is a worthwhile exercise when you are really trying to be fair to yourself. And it makes the path to younger parts of ourselves much easier to find.

I wonder if you have come to some knowledge of the part or parts of you that have been at the wheel of your life for a while. Inner child work has been around for a long time, and it's powerful work. As you look at your life and the decisions and choices that have landed you here at this time, I invite you to look for that part of you that might be doing all the work. You may find, as I did, that she wasn't very equipped to handle the situations you found yourself in. You might feel blame, disappointment and anger. You might feel overwhelmed by the task of reaching out to that inner you and helping to grow her up, but you have to do that. It's the only way to fully heal and become whole.

IT'S ALL ABOUT THE GRIEF

As I spend time alone, dissolving into the mush within my very own cocoon, sadness still hits me for all that I've lost. Although grief is not linear and we may circle through the stages over and over again, I have finally come to a place where I no longer am in denial of what happened or angry at the people involved. I have even let go of the anger I had for myself. I have cried until my eyes were swollen shut, ranted and raved to the empty rooms of my house 'til my cat was afraid to be near me.

I know that there are five stages to grief. They are denial, anger, bargaining, sadness, and finally acceptance. I realize now that I was in denial for years about my marriage and my life. As I read my journals from years ago, I see how unhappy I was. I was bouncing back and forth from pretending to be okay by putting my head in the sand and looking at my life through rose-colored glasses. I was always willing to shoulder the problems and accept the blame so that I could create peace—but at such a cost. Even after I found out about the affair, I still begged him to come back. I was that afraid of being alone, failing my marriage, avoiding the changes that were necessary for me to live the life I have always dreamed of.

Of course there was anger. I've already shared that. But it wasn't just at him or her. It was anger toward myself for wasting so much of my life, for not leaving sooner before losing so much. I would calm down and accept and then get angry again. What a cycle.

I spent a year trying to find a way to make my marriage work after the affair. Bargaining was a constant companion, offering all I could and asking for something in return only to be rejected time after time. I moved to a new town because I knew I needed space and time away, and yet I still hoped for the impossible—only to be disappointed.

And then... I hit the sadness with a vengeance. Honestly, I felt very sorry for myself. I had so few friends, spent so much time alone, and it rained all the time. The weather matched my moods, and in a way, it was kind of healing. I had to find my way back to a life. I was fortunate I didn't have to work unlike so many other women in my situation, but I did work part time just to get out of the house. I was very lonely, but resisted reaching out because having fun was the last thing I imagined doing.

I had no passion for life. I was just going through the motions every day. This went on for quite a while until finally I got sick and tired of being sick and tired of my life.

That's when I realized I was at a *choice point*. What is a choice point you ask? It is a moment in time when life offers you an opportunity to create two outcomes. One is the same old thing—the exact outcome you've always gotten, the crazy making circle of frustration you've traveled before landing you in the same place as always. The other is? Yup, you guessed it...*something different!*

That's really what it all comes down to. In every day, in every situation, in every relationship, and in every conversation, you have the opportunity to change your life. Like so many of the greats have said before:

If you don't like your reality...change your current thoughts.

If you feel stuck in your life or relationships...change your behavior.

When you change your thoughts and behaviors, your feelings change too.

Over time by varying your experiences, incorporating new data, and adding consistent practice, your thoughts will change, as well as your behaviors, your reality, and most importantly, your beliefs. You will have chosen "the road less traveled," and it *will* make all the difference.

After years of experiences, of dealing with my own set of beliefs, conditioned thoughts, and old behavior patterns, this is what I've come to understand. Ninety percent of everything we do (our behaviors) are driven by our unconscious beliefs. In order to change those beliefs, we must change our behavior and try something new. In other words, we must act as if those underlying beliefs driving our behaviors and thoughts that give us outcomes we do not desire are not true. I remember the first time I actually consciously did something different as if it were yesterday.

I was having a text conversation with him, in which—as was typical—he was making comments that left me feeling rejected, undervalued, and disrespected. My response in the past had always been to point out what he was doing in an attempt to get him to feel empathy and be kinder (which made him angrier). Alternatively, I'd respond with my own angry and defensive words (which only escalated the situation).

On that day, something inside me said, "STOP!" I heard myself say, "You know how this will end. Nothing is going to change by playing out this scene again and again." I continued thinking, "Yes, he is rejecting you and disrespecting you, but...." and this was a big one... "BUT you are rejecting and disrespecting yourself even more by continuing this pattern!"

WOW! That was a biggie for me. That instant I put down the phone, and I didn't communicate with him for several days. Trust me, it wasn't easy. It took every ounce of willpower, courage, and a lot of empowering self-talk to act in such an uncharacteristic way. I had no idea what the outcome of this doing "something different" would be, but I knew what the outcome of the "same old thing" would be—and I was done with that.

I was at a choice point, and I did something different.

I really believe that in some ways we humans are creatures of habit even when things don't serve us. We sometimes fight or in some way disrespect ourselves in order to keep a job we hate, a relationship that is abusive, or a habit that hurts us, all because we would rather deal with "the devil we know, than the one we don't." I know I've done this many, many times. But in the end, we are left with the same result—the same outcome, the same old...you know!

Unless we have the courage to DO something different!

At first, it will be uncomfortable, unfamiliar, maybe even difficult. But it is the only way to ultimately have an opportunity to change your outcome into the experience you want. You will have to override your conditioned responses to external events and stimuli by doing something different: different from your usual reaction, your usual behavior, your usual feeling. In doing so, you will create new neural pathways that over time will override the old habitual responses and generate this "something different" as automatically and comfortably as you used to do the old pattern. And no matter the situation or the external outcome, the ultimate result will be self-respect and self-love. And I believe that is actually what we want the most.

So, I was at a choice point. I could stay stuck forever in all the drama of a life that ultimately didn't serve me, or I could accept, finally, that it was over and really start to live again. So I chose to accept that my old life was over, and as I did, I found that I could actually allow myself to remember the good times. I could see a picture or an object, drive by an old stomping ground or hear a song, and I no longer cried. It didn't hurt to say his name, or her name for that matter. No one, not even him, could take away the life I knew.

I was so convinced that his treatment of me—the way it all ended—made 18 years of my life one big fat lie. But now, I know that isn't true. I'm the only one who can negate my experience by refusing to let go of what I wanted it to be. Instead, I saw what it was: the good, the bad and the ugly. And I was okay with it. I had finally come through the grief process to the place of acceptance. But this is what it took for me to get there. I had to look at what acceptance really was to me.

When we talk about acceptance, what we are really saying is: let it go, know that someday understanding will come and move on. Right? Because we aren't saying that what happened—what someone did or said to us—is favorable. In fact, we cannot condone acts that impact us negatively. We have to say, "This is not okay."

I know you will agree that sometimes things happen that lead to an outcome that we feel we consciously did not create—that we worked very hard to avoid. An outcome arrived that left us in a place, feeling a feeling, taking actions, thinking thoughts that we did not want. And sometimes it was not us that instigated it, so we feel victimized and want to understand why this happened. And we can't accept it until we do.

We are in pain, feel stuck, can't stop the thoughts circling in our brain incessantly looking for the answers to questions like:

How did this happen?

How could I not have known or anticipated?

What did I do wrong to deserve this?

How can I fix it?

How do I ever trust anyone or myself again?

You get the picture, right? But here's what I've figured out. Acceptance is not about condoning, understanding, or making things right again. It is simply about letting go: letting go of the need to know; letting go of the need to change things; letting go of an old plan, old dream, old way of being in favor of something new that has yet to come; and letting go of what you think should or would be happening right now "if only" and being okay in the present moment with what is.

It's kind of like what you do when you are watching a movie or reading a book, and half way through, you realize you are not enjoying it. So you simply turn off the T.V. or place the book back on the shelf. And instead of ruminating about why you didn't like it or how it didn't live up to your expectations, or calling friends to share your disappointment, you simply look around and ask yourself, "What now?" And maybe you sit for a while until the "what's next" shows up. And while you wait, you close your eyes, take some deep breaths, and you relax.

However, the grieving process does not end there, not really. For as you empty yourself of all that was, a space inside of you, which has been made empty, begs to be filled. The Universe abhors a vacuum and therefore will fill it. The question is with what?

Some people fill it with food, others with clothes, some with sex and relationships. Perhaps that's why 80% of all relationships are rebounds?

Well, I don't want to unconsciously fill that vacuum. I'm determined to fill it myself, consciously. My days, my time, my life will be replenished with the people, things, and opportunities I desire. At this point, I'm not sure exactly what to fill it with or with whom, but I am open to the possibilities. I feel it's time. So although I still have a long way to go—still feel that the old me is slowly dissolving into the potential I shall become—somehow, I feel a little stronger. I feel that destiny is at play, and I am riding an accelerated train to an unknown destination that promises....

Who knows what! And it doesn't matter. I just know that it will be better than where I came from. The void no longer scares me. I hope you have come to a place where you too are at least a little more comfortable with not knowing YET!

INSIGHTS:

I have known women with similar stories stay stuck for so long that they missed opportunities for something new and loving to enter their lives. As a result, they still sit in that lonely place of wondering when they will feel happy again. I don't want to miss that window when it opens.

I know that what has happened hurt you deeply, turned

your life upside down, and made you question everything you thought you knew. I know. I was stuck in the pain for a while. And when I allowed myself to feel the feelings completely, grieve fully, and really let go, I found a sense of peace. The questions in my head stopped. The dust settled, and I slowly saw what my next step might be. I gently nudged myself into a new life.

I also found that—although I knew I didn't consciously create it—my experience was exactly what I needed to have happen to grow into my highest potential. Over time, I knew I would be able to look into the old situation with clarity and accept that I was unconsciously participating in the "something" that happened. And that's when the greatest letting go occurred. I let go of blaming myself and others, and I saw the truth, the authenticity of my experience. In other words, I had finally accepted and forgiven myself. That has to happen…before you can truly forgive anyone else!

How Do I Forgive?

Forgiveness is a funny thing. Well, maybe funny isn't the right word. People talk and teach about forgiveness all the time—how it's not about condoning the other person's behavior but letting go of something. Anger? Rage? I'm not sure. They say it is about loving the person who wronged you anyway, of rising above, and so many other—dare I say clichés?

Once I had a reading from a man who channeled the Arcturians, you know, the blue people from Avatar. I admit I am being playful here, but stay with me. The world famous Edgar Cayce, a prophet who lived from 1877-1945, was quoted as remarking, "Arcturus is the highest civilization in our galaxy." Cayce spoke frequently about alien life forms visiting Earth in many of his writings. He believed the Arcturians to be a "fifth- dimensional" life form that are highly-advanced, both technically and spiritually. I'm not saying for sure this is all true, but it is interesting.

The man I saw was able to shift his consciousness and allow these beings to come through him. The Arcturians were offering those who came to see them insights about the seekers' gifts. Now I know some people would say that this is woo-woo, crazy stuff. But at the time of my reading, a lot of what they said to me and others present really fit.

I was told that I am the Empress of Forgiveness. What! I know that sounds weird. But when I look at my life from the time I was a child, I realize that I've had a lot of practice. He said that I had the gift of helping others to find the stone of resentment within their bodies and remove it. I actually tried playing with this idea with some clients who were game. I was surprised when I was able to intuit where they held their anger and pain in their bodies. I could sense what had happened, what the story was, and they confirmed my findings. I'm not sure I really removed it from them, but it was an interesting experience for all of us. And when I went back to my journals, I found this passage channeled one year earlier:

This message today is for you, Our Dear, but eventually, you will write for others so that your words, our words, shall inspire and wake up, open and release, and free the heart to its full nature, its full glory. Only through the power of forgiveness, which is the true power of love, can this be so. And you know, it starts with love of self. For only when all truly know that their heart is full to the brim with self-love, with the knowledge of connection to All-ness, can they truly be free to know the oneness and connection to each other. The time is now. The time has come. And many, many know this. They sense it, and they are ready. Imagine how beautiful it will be when all can know instantly what is real and true, when all will have open hearts and sing with joy the praises of this life experience without self-judgement or judgement of others. This is what you know. You feel it like a pinprick every time you sense judgement coming from another, when their words reveal the pain they carry. And your ears perk up to the incongruence of their thoughts. Like a light that has just been shone on a dark spot, you see with your eyes that which clearly shows through the others' eyes: the call for help, for understanding and for guidance.

Funny how this channeled writing came once again just before my greatest challenge occurred—a message perhaps of the forgiveness work I'd first be doing with myself.

I have never been one to hold a grudge. I really can't stay angry for long. Maybe it is because I yearn so much to connect with others that staying angry just seems counter-intuitive to what I want.

Regardless, I recognize that many times in my life when others have talked about forgiveness, something inside me would get irritated. At those times, I never understood why. What I heard from others was that forgiveness was an act that you could simply choose to perform, and that didn't sit well with me.

Now, after all I've been through, I know that forgiveness is not something you do. It's not something you simply decide. It's not something you think your way through. Forgiveness is the natural outcome of letting go: letting go of being right, of expecting something to change, of trying to control a situation, of allowing the process of grief to fully run its course until you come to the place of acceptance. It is acceptance of what is, of what happened, of what you thought would be that never will.

When I get to that place of forgiveness, I feel at peace. No longer do I experience the tightness in my throat, the quickening of my breath, the anxiety in my gut, or the fear in my heart when I am in the presence of the one who has hurt me. Whether the injury is slight or huge, I find myself at ease. In other words, it is my body that tells me I have done the work.

Time doesn't heal all wounds...but the work to heal takes time. There is no right time, and it cannot be forced. You can try and convince yourself that you have forgiven, but until you have felt that feeling of ease rush through your body like liquid gold, forgiveness hasn't truly happened yet. Now mind you, you can forgive, but that doesn't mean you forget. And it doesn't mean that when you remember it doesn't hurt anymore. Let's be clear about that.

It simply means you no longer feel the need to make it right, control it, change it, or even understand it.

I remember the first time I recognized what this feeling felt like. We had bought into a franchise and invested almost everything we had. There were 28 other families who had done the same. We all believed that the owners of this franchise were acting in good faith, had something of value that we could all participate in, and wanted everyone's success. But within a year of our investment, they closed the doors and took everyone's money with them. Needless to say, we were angry. We brought a lawsuit against them which took three years to settle. By that time, the money was gone, and we all lost.

I grieved for all the things I had lost for a while. I went through all the stages and came out the other side acknowledging their part in this mess and taking responsibility for mine.

I remember the day that I faced these men in court and how I felt nothing but compassion for them and for us all. My body was at ease. When they apologized, I was able to look them in the eyes and honestly say, "I accept your apology."

I've talked a lot about my now ex-husband and the feelings I went through to get my divorce. However, I haven't shared much about the other betrayal, the one that hurt perhaps even more—the betrayal and loss of my best friend. And I want to share a special encounter, one that I feel was divinely orchestrated.

But to truly share this amazing experience, I must backtrack. Twenty-five years ago when my first husband, four little kids, and I moved from Southern California to Oregon, I left the warmth and safety of my family for the first time in my life. They were no longer there to share in the rearing of my children, to celebrate the daily triumphs over a meal, to encourage new opportunities, or hold me when I needed comforting. I had only my husband and children to do those things with and for me.

Until one day at a PTA meeting, this beautiful blond woman, towering five inches above me, protested angrily over something I had brought up in that session. I was immediately enthralled by her and intimidated. It's a weird way to start a relationship, I admit. But start one we did.

We got through that initial conversation, and within weeks, she quickly became my best friend. Our husbands enjoyed each other's company too, and we found ourselves spending much of our free time together: playing games, tending children, listening to music, and sharing our dreams.

Our children also became best friends. We spent holidays together: searching for Easter eggs, carving the turkey, and singing Christmas carols. We home-schooled our kids together, even raised 4-H pigs; and her extended family eventually became my new one. We could talk for hours on any subject. We laughed until we peed on ourselves and cried desperate tears when sharing our common childhood traumas. In short, she was my soul sister.

It was she who reminded my first husband of our anniversary, she who stood by my side as I made the decision to leave my marriage. And it was she who was my matron of honor when I married my next husband with whom she later had an affair.

Over the years as our children grew and our lives changed, she and her family were still a huge part of my life. She worked for me in several of my businesses, and I was there for her when her husband broke his back falling off a roof at work. Although our lives sometimes took us on different paths, we still saw each other every week at bowling and had our monthly afternoon teas where we shared our deepest wants and hurts.

It was to her that I confided the angsts in my new marriage: the pain of rejection, the lack of communication, the feeling of disconnection. There were many times over the years that she told me to leave him and that I deserved better. So you can imagine the depth of my pain when I found out it was her that my husband was cheating with.

I'll never forget that day.

One look at our phone bill told me the ominous truth. After he and I had a horrible fight and he had not come home for three days, I'd found he'd been texting and talking with her during that time. So I did what anyone would do. I called her asking what was going on. She said, "We are just friends, and he's been unhappy," to which I replied, "Okay, but you know I've been unhappy too, and you haven't called me?"

Something in her voice and explanation sent the alarm bells in my head tolling. Fear crept into my heart which was pounding so hard I thought I'd have a heart attack. Nothing she was saying made sense.

"Did you know he was leaving me?" I asked.

And she said yes.

So I replied, "I can't understand how as my best friend you wouldn't have called and prepared me for this."

Her answer astounded me. "That's your problem. You think everyone owes you." With that statement, I knew something terrible was happening.

I hung up and went back to scouring the phone bills. That's when I saw that the texts went back for months— all the way back through my birthday, Christmas... Valentine's Day. These texts went on every day for a year, from ten to fifty times a day. Even in the middle of the night while I slept.

I felt like I had been spun out to space, some foreign place where nothing was real, nothing made sense, and from which I would never find my way back to solid ground. My best friend! My soul sister! My confidante! She had stepped into my life in a way she had no right to do, and she'd broken my heart.

The affair ended the same day I found out, when I let her husband know what was going on. She did all she could to save her marriage because leaving her husband for mine was never her intent. Still I couldn't understand what or why she had done what she'd done.

I tried to see her six weeks later. She refused to talk to me then. She promised she'd call in three days and then had her husband call me and tell me to stay away. Once more, I was confused and hurt. I was the victim here! I hadn't done anything. Why was this happening?

I cried more then than I've cried all my life. I had lost something precious and didn't know why. And all I could do was try to accept it—an impossible task.

Eight months later, I received an email from her asking for forgiveness. In it, she said she was guilty of "abandoning our relationship without explanation" and of "not telling the truth at times that would have made the ending easier." What!??? "No," I screamed as I read it, "you were guilty of an affair with my husband!"

I didn't respond to the letter for six months. And when I did, I sent an audio email. I shared how devastated I was, how much I loved her, how angry I was at what she did, and how much I missed her. During that time, I could hardly say her name without palpitations. I realized that so much of my life's memories included her, and it hurt to remember. More than anything, I wanted to know "why." What had I done to make her hate me so much that she could lie to my face for a year, pretending to be my friend? During the time she was having the affair with my husband, we saw each other every week. I helped her with her son's wedding. She and her family were at my Christmas gathering. She and her husband came to our house many times for an evening of dinner and a soak in the hot tub. All that time, she and my husband were meeting publicly, kissing, and texting, even while I was in their presence. One time, after a fight with my husband, she came over to console me and did a Tarot reading in which she said my marriage was over, and I'd be getting a divorce in six weeks— this while she was having an affair with him. It was five months from that evening before I found out about it.

My mind reels when I remember all this, my body memory of that fateful day still lingering in my racing heart and tense muscles. But I no longer feel the pain or anger. I feel I've accepted that I will never understand, and that is okay. As time passed, I allowed myself to surrender to the feeling of missing my friend. Slowly, I found that I could say her name in connection with my life stories, which for 24 years she and her family were a part of, without hurting. Sometimes, I would actually laugh out loud as I recalled some past event we shared, and I'd be pleasantly surprised. It's weird how the mind can do that.

Four months after sending her the audio email, I went back to my hometown to get my divorce, and a miracle occurred.

I had planned a day of visits with family and friends, driving from one end of town to another. At one point, I questioned myself about my plans, thinking perhaps I'd chosen to do too many things in one day. But Spirit had other plans, and I heard a resounding "No" in my head when I thought about changing them.

After visiting with my kids, I drove out to the country, where years before I hung out each day with my friend and our kids. There, I met another old friend I hadn't seen in years. The plan was to go for an hour walk, then go to a small cafe and have coffee. That was our plan, but Spirit had another. After a sequence of inconsequential delays, we went to the cafe just as it closed. The lady there said there was a street fair going on, and perhaps we'd find coffee there. So off we went.

After parking, I turned to my friend just as we began to enter the street fair saying, "You know, she could be here. She only lives a few blocks away." To which my friend replied, "Oh my God, should we leave?"

And at that very moment, I felt her. I turned my

head and said "It's too late. There she is." It was as if time stood still. We made eye contact, and I could see the apprehension in her eyes, followed by a smile of recovery. My body took over before I even had a chance to think, and I walked right up to her. She was with other people, some who knew me and others who knew of me. I said hello, and so did she. Then I asked her if she'd gotten my email, and she said she had and was going to write me back but wanted to be sure to say it all "right." Hmmm.

I nodded and said I only wanted to know one thing. Why?

Her answer was that she was "fucked up" and that she'd been in therapy for over a year figuring it all out. I asked if she'd thought of me when she was having the affair, and she said "every day." Hmmm.

The whole thing was surreal. Her answers really weren't explaining anything, and for some reason, it didn't seem to matter. This woman, whom I loved and shared so many things with, was standing in front of me for the first time in over a year, and all I could feel were the years of love for her flowing through me.

I wasn't afraid, wasn't shaking, wasn't angry. When she said she really couldn't talk right then because people were waiting for her and promised to call me, I simply said yes. Then I stepped toward her with open arms, my body moving once again of its own accord.

She fell into my arms, and immediately we both started crying—crying for what we'd lost and crying with relief to once again be in each other's embrace. She whispered in my ear over and over again, "I'm sorry." And I whispered back, "I know, and I forgive you."

I felt all the questions that had run through my mind over the last year drain out of me with every tear. I felt a warm glow in my heart as I released all the pain. In that split second, the grieving was done and forgiveness had happened. It was so beautiful, so tender, and so divinely orchestrated.

As we unlocked our embrace, I told her I'd always known that once I saw her I'd forgive her because although I was devastated by what she'd done, 24 years of sisterhood—of love, of sharing our lives—just couldn't be wiped away. To try to do that, to invalidate all we'd been to each other, would have made all those years a lie. It would have discounted all that we'd learned and who we'd grown to be. And that was something I wasn't willing to do.

I asked her if there was anything I'd done to hurt her, and she said, "No, you never did anything but love me." With those words my own doubt in myself also was released. I had loved her well. Her actions were not something I deserved in some way. When I told her I was getting a divorce, she nodded and then said two more things.

"Seeing you hurting in that relationship with him over the last five years was so painful. He is an evil man."

"Yes he is," I said. With that she looked deeply into my eyes, turned her head slightly away, then back. In that instant, I knew what she was thinking. After all, we had spent 24 years together finishing each other's sentences, exploring our belief systems, sharing our pain and our joys. So it didn't surprise me to see in her eyes that we were both remembering a story we'd heard told long ago, by Neal Donald Walsh.

It was the story of a little soul in Heaven talking to God and asking to come to Earth to experience humanness. God replied that it was fine, but to truly know all of the human story, learn about human nature, and feel the ecstasy of emotions, she would need an adversary, one who would come just to test her and provide the lessons she wanted. Right then, another soul stepped up and agreed to play the role but with one request, that the little soul remember this agreement and know it was entered into with love.

When we heard that story, we both cried. Having had similar experiences in our childhood with our fathers who shared the same first name, we had come to accept that their roles as adversaries were part of an agreement we made with them so that we could become who we were. Somehow that story made sense to us. It shed the feelings of blame and provided a sacred space of letting go of the pain.

And in that moment, as we stood in the street, looking into each other's eyes, I could sense that story reverberating in both of us. I simply said, "I know," and she nodded. With one last embrace, we parted ways. She had said she'd call but never did, and I was okay with that. We'd done what we needed to do. Our story was over, as was our journey in this lifetime.

Forgiveness occurred and I walked away feeling like I'd been given the most exquisite gift from God. I could sense the hand of Spirit in every word, every nuance, every touch. And I was filled with gratitude—gratitude for the experience, but even more for the awareness of the durability and flexibility of the human heart...for the grace that I felt in knowing that I am never alone. For the magic that is life itself.

I can't say that I still don't wonder at times what she's doing, whether she misses me, or even occasionally why she did it. But I can say that I no longer feel desperately sad or angry. Now it's just a soft question, and the soft answer is...it doesn't matter. Life moves on.

And today, I know that I have a choice: to stay stuck and blame, to stay fearful and separate from my true nature, to crumble to pieces and give up, to close up and protect my heart, or to remain powerless and paralyzed.

Or...I can let go, forgive, accept, appreciate, and finally truly love myself and live my purpose. But to do this, I have to allow myself to really feel the feelings, not submerge them deeply into my unconscious where they fester and ultimately control my behaviors. That is the true choice. To feel and heal, then act from my highest potential, or to suppress and unconsciously express by manifesting all that I don't want.

I don't know about you, but I want the first choice. I want something good to come out of all that has been so devastating. I want to believe that everything that happened occurred for a reason. So that's what we are going for here.

So I guess my heart is still open even after all I've been through. Perhaps *I am* the Empress of Forgiveness! Or maybe, I am just a woman evolving into a more consciously loving human. Perhaps I'm stepping into my fullest potential?

In my journal, I found these two astrological readings, shortly after the message I channeled which I shared earlier. It was for the first two days in February. They read as follows:

February 1. Venus is in opposition to Mars. The tendency will be to feel like a victim of the universe. After all, you have been diligently working the principles of the Law of Attraction and instead of more money coming in, your car breaks down, and you have no money to get it fixed. You start to believe that you cannot manifest your dreams. Pay attention to the events that are creating obstacles in your life. They are showing you a belief that you have that is stopping you. When setbacks no longer bother you, they will stop coming into your life.

And...

February 3. Neptune moves into Pisces and will be there until 2025. The challenge with Neptune is that it will bring illusion, confusion, and deception, and at the same time spirituality, awakening and inspiration. Neptune also dissolves the limitations of Saturn. In the area of spirituality, what you think you believe about God, Life, and the Universe will be challenged if you are simply regurgitating dogma and teachings, no matter how noble and altruistic, that you have acquired over the years. Your truth must come from you. So put the books away and find out what you really believe because the events you will experience this upcoming year will make you do that. Another area that Neptune in Pisces will affect is forgiveness. All the information you are receiving is that there is no such thing as forgiveness. There is nothing to forgive because if you resonate in that belief, then you are saying that something is/was wrong and that sets up resistance to what you want to experience. So, along with karma, forgiveness must be put to rest for you to reach your full potential. There is nothing to forgive. There is only love.

Hmmm. Well that kind of sums it up. When I read that back then, I had no idea what was coming into my life. I can see how I resisted the teachings my soul was yearning for. I put myself through way more than I needed to, but in the end, that's okay. I'm here now. Still not clear where I'm heading, but I am clear that it is and will be better than where I was. They say hindsight is 20/20. I'm living proof. My life would certainly be different today had I not had all those experiences.

I know I have yet to forgive him completely. He continues to create stress in my life, even after the divorce. It's like I have a wound that is partially healed, and he keeps picking at the scab. But it is me who allows it. After feeling the relief that forgiving her gave me, I want more than anything to feel that for him. Not for his sake, but for mine. To some degree, I do forgive him the things he has done in the past. But I also now know that I have to remain vigilant in my present. I cannot let myself forget who he really is because although I can forgive him, he is still the same man. I know I cannot trust him, but I'm learning to trust myself again. And that is huge!

We can and do take on more responsibility than we have to as women. I think we are wired for that, perhaps so that we can have the patience and willingness to sacrifice ourselves for our children. We do the best we can. And sometimes we do screw up. But just as we would forgive our children and love them no matter what, we have to learn to do that for ourselves. Holding ourselves hostage to our past with self-blame only keeps us from who we are capable of being. It stops the flow of creativity, of passion, of the brilliance that we are capable of.

There's still work to do. But each day, I feel I get closer to it—closer to me, closer to a vision of my new life. I wonder where you are in the process? Are you ready to let it all go? To allow the grief to move through you like a clear crystal spring? I hope so.

I had an experience that changed my life— that catapulted me into the cocoon. I have changed. Transformed. Become anew. Through this experience, I have done a lot of healing of very old wounds. I have let go of a lot of co-dependent behaviors. I have learned to be good company to myself. And what I feel is hopeful— hopeful that there is really a life for me out there. Oh, I still am occasionally sad, and sometimes a little scared. I am still feeling a little adrift at sea, still praying and looking for signs that I'm on the right path. But now, the only voice in my head is my own. Now, the tunnel is behind me, the light so close I can almost touch it. So close...

INSIGHTS:

I believe that when we are betrayed...when we lose something important to us...when things don't work out the way we dreamed them to be...when someone has really let us down... forgiveness isn't simply a choice.

That was not my experience. After working with my clients, I am pretty sure it wasn't their experience either. When we suffer these things, it is easy and natural to go to the place of shame and blame. In order to come back from that place, we have to feel safe. And safety is usually the first thing that is stripped from us in times of transition and transformation.

So how do we reclaim that sense of safety?

It starts with acknowledging our pain and releasing our anger...

...then it is about revisiting the story only long enough to see that what we have lost through this experience is our ability to trust ourselves and others and our personal power...

...and then we reclaim it...

...we make the decision to do something different from our old patterns...

...that's when we are able to see our choices and begin to act with love for self...

...take responsibility for our part no matter how small...

...and safety is returned.

That's when the magic happens…when we accept where we landed. We are able to forgive ourselves, find the gems in the experience, and finally forgive others too. We know forgiveness has happened because we no longer have a visceral feeling in our body. Remember our body cannot lie. It will let us know if we still feel unsafe (forgiveness hasn't happened) or feel completely safe (forgiveness has occurred). It's really that simple.

PART III

THE BUTTERFLY...
NEW BEGINNINGS

When the transformation is complete, like the butterfly, we rejoin the world anew. As we emerge, changed from the inside, we are still tentative at first. Our new wings—new ways—are still fragile and need time to get strong. Empowered by the grace of our own inner journey, we practice testing our wings. The more we become accustomed to them, the more ready we are to start our new adventure, as a whole new person at the threshold of a new way to live.

Hanging Upside Down

H ere I am again writing in the middle of the night. I can't tell you what exactly wakes me up, only that I can't go back to sleep. It's not a bad thing though. I love writing when the world is asleep, sharing my thoughts, and watching the light on the horizon bring on the new day. And there have been a lot of "new" days since I've last written. In many ways, I have experienced "new" parts of me too.

Six months has gone by since my attorney took over communicating with my ex about the business. It cost me a lot of money, but it saved my sanity. He continued to respond through his attorney in ways that were less than civil, doing things that were less than ethical. During that time, I allowed her to handle everything with him, and I began to feel impatient.

My life, although a lot more peaceful now, seems to be going nowhere. I still can't see a vision of my future clearly, but at least I can feel one beginning to take shape.

I've joined some women's groups and made some really nice friends. I've always been a leader, and this opportunity allowed me to reconnect with that part of myself that loves to teach and share with others.

While talking with so many women about their experience after a difficult divorce or breakup, I found that one of two things happens pretty often. Either they jump right back into a new relationship within months of the separation, or they hide from another relationship for so long that sometimes years and years go by without even a date. There's a lot of popular advice about knowing the right timing to get back out in the world of relationship, but I think each of us has to make that decision for ourselves. There is no right or wrong way to re-enter the world as a single woman.

But it is scary, isn't it? Since I was 20 years old, there have been two men in my life, and both of them were husbands. When I look back, I realize how young I was, especially now that my kids have reached that age. I thought I was such a grown-up making grown-up decisions. And today, I feel more like a kid than I did then.

I have gone out with the girls and watched couples from my age group. It's weird how, when you are married for a long time, you don't really see the aging process taking place in your spouse. Somehow in your mind, they are still as young as the day you met them. But being single in my late 50's, I have to say, it is shocking how old the men out there look. I'm sure they feel the same when they look at us women, which is why they want the younger ones. It scares me that I don't feel attraction. I can't help but wonder if it is my age or my fear of being hurt again…or my doubts about myself…or… You get the picture.

So of course at this point, I get hypercritical about my looks. Who's going to want me? Can they tell I've been damaged? Am I ready for a relationship or am I just needing to feel the attention of a man to assuage the hurt of knowing my ex is now in his second relationship since our divorce? Am I being fair to a man I might meet? Will I really be present to him or am I just proving something to myself? Wow, I know you have these thoughts, too. Be honest. And know that it's all okay. On the other side of fear is hope. And hope is a good thing.

I can understand given how I'm feeling why women of my age find it hard to get back out in the dating world. But like falling off a horse, you have to get back out there before too much time has gone by, or you might give up on love forever. I've seen that happen. I know I'd be okay alone, but I also know I miss having someone with whom to share my day, cuddle in front of the fire, plan a trip, and so much more.

Since I work from home and live in a new town, my chances of meeting someone through my social network or work world are pretty slim. So I did what so many other women are doing. I got online.

Now that's a weird world to step into. There are so many sites—many free—where page after page of people are sharing who they are with total strangers. It's like applying to a blind job advertisement. It's hard to know what to say about yourself. It's a one way conversation.

You are selling yourself to someone you don't know, but it's a sell that everyone gets to see.

For me, the hardest part is that there is no context for "this guy." In other words, I'm not meeting him through a trusted friend, work environment, or through common interests like golfing, bowling, or book club! These are the old fashioned ways we used to meet, and there was at least some element of commonality at the start. Online it starts with reading a profile and hoping what has been said is the truth. You can imagine how difficult that is for me given I just came out of an 18 year relationship full of deceit, unsure if I can rely on my own judgement. So once again, it comes down to self-trust.

Do I trust myself enough: to know what I want and not settle for less, to take care of myself and get out early if the clues are there that this is not good, and to take my time to fall in love? I have to admit I'm scared. But there's only one way to find out the answers to those questions, right?

So, I began saying yes to "flirts" and to coffee dates. I met several men, all of whom were very sweet and professed their love for me on the second date! My radar was up. It would have been so easy to get on that train. Honestly, it felt great to be adored, especially after being so rejected by my ex. But something about it also felt unhealthy.

For me, sex and love always walked hand in hand. That's not a bad thing—except when sex came first or at least too early for love to be true. When that happened in the past, my inner child would convince herself that she was in love so that I could feel the sex act was wholesome. One of the things I experienced very early in this new dating scene was that men wanted sex and intimacy right away. Some part of me needed to know I was sexually attractive, especially given how my marriage had ended with the worst of rejections. However, many of these men had some kind of erectile dysfunction, which I found interesting given that was the one area my ex and I had no problem in.

My girlfriends told me it's our age. My inner child told me it was me. My wise, higher self said, "Girl, you are attracting these men." And so I had to ask myself why.

The simple answer—I was still not ready for a relationship. I was still not clear about what I wanted from a relationship, still not sure about who I was when I was in one. I can't help but wonder if the sex was great would I have gotten into a long-term relationship with one of these men, even though I knew they weren't right for me?

I did date two guys for a couple months, not at the same time. Both were not from an online dating site. Both were introduced to me through people I trusted, which made them seem safer. One was tender, loving, kind, and fun. He really treated me like a lady: opening doors, paying for dinners and trips. But as time went by, I started seeing a neediness and insecurity in him that I didn't want to deal with. I found myself stepping into old patterns again of putting his needs ahead of my own, of accepting his excuses despite my desires, of taking care of him instead of myself. Ooops!

The great thing is that I saw it. I saw myself. I recognized early my "fix it" mentality, and I got out. That was a great learning experience of stepping into my truth, of acting on behalf of me. Yup, that was good.

Then the other guy showed up. At first, it was exciting. He was poetic and sensual. We shared the experience of a sudden suicide by a dear friend that brought us closer out of a need to comfort each other through the loss. But over time, I saw that this man was "all about himself." He'd show up uninvited from out of town and expected me to open my home, my kitchen, and my bed to him. Something about it all felt intrusive, but so many of my friends liked this man that I found myself discounting my feelings about him and taking on the opinions of others. Oops again!

Once again, I ended the relationship quickly. I was proud of myself for holding healthy boundaries, and I am grateful to both of them because I learned some very important things about myself through my experiences of them.

I learned that I need a strong man who is gentle: one who is confident about himself without arrogance; one who is spiritual but grounded; one who is intelligent, creative, and resourceful but has nothing to prove to anyone.

I also learned that sex and love don't have to be forever. You can love someone and not be in a committed relationship. And you can have sex and not give away your soul. I have learned to be whole without a man. I don't need one to complete me or to give me substance.

As I discovered myself in the context of these new relationships, I realized I was no longer lonely. I realized that being alone didn't mean that I wasn't loved or cherished. Having sex with someone I wasn't in a committed relationship with didn't mean I was a tramp. I wasn't selling my body for love, and I wasn't selling my soul with my body.

There is a very powerful feeling of internal stability that comes with this newfound experience of me. Do I want a relationship? Am I ready for one?

I think the answer is yes. And I am willing to wait for the right one to come. I trust that it will and that I will know it when it presents itself. It will not begin nor be sustained by need, fear, turning a blind eye to that which I don't want, or by changing who I am to accommodate what is offered. I am so clear on this.

I know it's hard to look back at all that's happened in your relationship: the lies, the deceit, the constant maneuvering of trying to find safety, the denial in order to make peace, and the sellout of your soul trying to elicit love. It's hard to trust that you won't fall into the same patterns again. Right?

What I have come to realize is that trusting myself will never fully happen if I don't take some responsibility for what happened to me. If I make it all about him and how he couldn't be trusted, then it means that I have to find someone who is totally trustworthy so it doesn't happen again. And that might prove very difficult because there is no perfect person out there. There are certainly some that are better than others, but how will I know which one I end up with? I know I don't want to live in a place of constant suspicion in order to keep myself safe, always wondering if I'm getting told the truth.

What it comes down to is this: no matter what he did, I was the one who allowed it. By allowing it, I was the one harming myself. I had convinced myself that I allowed it because I loved him. But I now see that's not true. My "love" for him was just as unhealthy as his "abuse" was of me.

Knowing this now—accepting this now—makes all the difference. Now that I am conscious, no longer acting from the hidden parts of me, I will be creating consciously that which I want rather than that which I don't want. And I am willing to wait expectantly for it because I know that love is real. I know that love is the only thing that survives when fear dies. And I am no longer afraid...

INSIGHTS:

One of the things I believe to be important as you step out into the dating scene is that you remember you are a very young butterfly...wings still damp from the birthing process. Don't go out there looking for "the one." Not yet. When you begin to date, it's not about the guy. It's all about you. Treat this time as an experiment, a lab class where you are the one under the microscope. Put your attention on what you are feeling, acting, and thinking—not him. I was mindful of every nuance as I interacted in these relationships. I noticed my feelings and how I communicated them. I didn't make excuses for myself or for them. And I didn't try to make them into something they were not. In each case, I accepted what they offered and didn't try to change them or accommodate them by changing me. In other words, I was no longer co-dependent!

This is big. This is huge. This is what needs to happen for all of us who were once in relationships with narcissists, addicts, abusers, and otherwise unhealthy people. We have to come to terms with our own shadow, that deep, hurt part of ourselves that looks for healing in the actions of another. We have to take responsibility for our own well-being rather than look to someone else to fix us by loving us in unhealthy ways.

Also important at this stage of transformation is to beware of getting stuck in survival strategies. They are very seductive. Some of those strategies may be getting into a new relationship, finding a new job, adding a new hobby, moving to a new town. These strategies help us navigate in a world that has been turned upside down. But it's easy to believe that you have done the work when you find peace and solace in these activities.

So how will you know if you are stuck in survival strategies instead of something new and healthy? You'll know by how you feel when the "strategy" goes away. When the guy leaves, the job goes away, the newness wears off, the passion is gone… and you find yourself back in the feelings of the old story, trapped once again by the "what if" and "if only" mentality, then you have just been using a strategy. Use this information as a clue to what you need to do next, not as a means to beat yourself up.

Remember...you are a new butterfly. Give yourself grace and start looking for what is different in you that is worth expanding. Look to how you are loving, trusting, and forgiving yourself...again. And start experimenting once more...

MOUNTAINTOP WISDOM

OMG. I got away…I did it. I stood up for myself. I trusted my knowing for the first time ever! I'm at my friend's house looking out the window and enjoying the breeze coming off of the river. I feel elated—even though I'm couch-surfing, even though all I own is in storage because I don't have a place to live right now, even though I had to borrow money from my son to pay for the movers to carry my stuff away, even though I have no idea what is next. I am elated beyond measure. My smile feels like it's painted on. It's like the universe told a joke, and I got it. I feel like I just won a game of *Clue*. It was Ms. Penny in the library with the candlestick.

I know that all sounds almost silly, but really, I'm telling you this is a breakthrough moment. And it all started with a chat on Match! Oh yes, it's about a man. But I swear, sometimes my best learning comes from these relationships. So here goes!

This is one crazy story of a guy who lived on a mountain, knew all the right things to say, invited me to live with him and grow pot. Good grief, I don't even smoke the stuff. He had long hair and a mischievous smile. I'm sure all my friends and my kids thought I was crazy. But he told me the mountain healed him and could heal me too. When I'd go to visit we'd wake up at dawn and light candles, make a fire and listen to Ram Das. He was a Cordon Bleu trained chef, and we would dance in the candlelight as he made me seven-course gourmet meals. The land was remote, and the energy was either solar-powered or generator-driven. Wood fires kept us warm. Yoga, long walks amongst the Madrone trees, and talking of divine love all fed my heart. I was in heaven, surrounded by nature and feeling that Spirit had called me to make a home here with this man.

So when he asked me to move to the mountain with him, told me he loved me and wanted to marry me some day, well, of course I said yes. Who wouldn't! I was tired of being alone. It had been almost two years since my divorce. And my ex was long past his first girlfriend and on to his next. I was beginning to wonder what was wrong with me, once again falling into old habits of needing external validation to be ok with myself.

But it didn't matter now. He wanted me. And what a life I would have! He had done such a great job of showing me everything I needed to see to believe I was coming home to the life I dreamed of and believed I deserved.

But the day I moved in, unloaded the truck—strategically placing my furniture around the house and turning the space into a home—he changed: gone were the candles, the walks, and the dancing. The house became dark and sad, lonely and cold. He was obsessed with alien invasions, smoked pot constantly and added alcohol into the mix. Sometimes it was scary. I was very isolated up there. I was living with a stranger, and then every once in a while, I'd see the guy I'd been attracted to show up and ask for help, money, or something to put a smile on his face. I could feel myself slipping away, once again handing over what little I had, letting go of my work, making his needs more important than my own and letting cobwebs shut down my vision.

But here's the good news! I got away!!! It was like I suddenly woke up from a very bad dream, and—despite the fact that I'd told all my friends just two months earlier that I was with the man of my dreams, living the life I'd always wanted—I was able to recognize the signs that I was in an unhealthy relationship and abandoning myself once again.

But this time, I didn't wait. It didn't matter that I had no place to go, no money to even pay for the truck and movers. It didn't matter what other people thought. What mattered was that I saw it. I knew this was not ok. I knew who he was and that I would never change him. That unlike the situation with my last husband, when I believed that if I loved him enough, he'd love me back… this time I saw the guy in front of me and decided he's just not my guy!

As I drove away off that mountaintop—my car filled to the brim, not knowing what my next step was, where I'd land, who'd be there—I knew for certain what I had left behind was far worse than the unknown place I was going. The sun shone so brightly it almost blinded me. My eyes filled with tears of joy as I felt the connection with my soul. Unlike the last time I drove away, devastated and alone, this time I was grandly exhilarated.

I swear I heard a band of angels singing *Hallelujah!* It was magnificent. In that moment, I became my own best friend because I realized that I would never abandon myself again. This was a milestone on my road to transformation. He will never know how grateful I am to him. He was the man who woke up my inner guardian— the part of me that could look beyond the behaviors, the disappointments, the expectations, and just take care of me. I harbor no anger toward this man who taught me how to say YES to me.

As I sit here now, I feel gratitude and something else. I'm not sure what I'd call it. It feels like strength but not in the old way of being strong in the face of adversity. It feels like peace but not in the way that you feel when the work is over. I guess the best way to describe it is that the hole that has been a part of my heart for these last few years feels like it has gotten a little smaller. I don't feel like I'm leaking energy in all directions or trying like hell to contain it. I feel grounded, and that's different. I still have no idea what's coming or where I'm going...but as Scarlett O'Hara said, "I'm not going to think about that today...I'll think about that tomorrow."

Insights:

I think each of us needs one of these moments. After years of being absent to ourselves, of letting others' needs be more important, believing what others say about us, allowing others to manipulate us, and then beating ourselves up for all of it...we all need that experience when we realize we are not going to take it anymore. We all need that Norma Rae moment played by Sally Fields.

I know it's really scary to let yourself be that vulnerable again. I know many women will avoid it. But those who do hide from love will never find themselves in the dark. Because you see, we don't learn something once. We have to let our awareness of self grow by facing ourselves over and over again. And during that time, we must be kind to ourselves, or we will never find what we want. We have to go in there and get ourselves out. We have to stand up for ourselves in the way someone should have when we were little. It's not too late. Remember the saying...you will bloom when the pain of staying shut up in the cocoon becomes greater than what's on the outside. I'm ready...are you?

Who Knows Me Now?

I've landed. I'm now living in Portland with my daughter. We are the best of friends, but still, there is a little discomfort with saying I live with her. I am a grown woman after all. But the company is great, and it's giving me a chance to regroup. I've decided to go back into real estate, not because I love it, but because I'm good at it. I've been in and out of the industry for over 30 years. And I'm not sure I'm ready to help others with their problems through coaching and counseling quite yet. I have to be sure that my inner work is complete.

Right now, I'm sitting on the deck watching the pears fall to the ground. Far too many to eat, and I feel a little like those pears lying there waiting for someone to pick them up and enjoy their gift. In this moment, I realize how much I miss my old life—not the marriage, not the pain, but the sense of belonging.

I have made some new friends here in the valley, but what is so weird is that none of them "knew me when." It's like I was recently born, or landed here from another planet, and no one knows anything about me. My history hasn't followed me here—not my achievements or my failures. It's a weird feeling.

I have spent the last 25 years of my life in a small town that grew around me. Over time, I had become kind of a big fish in a small pond. My friends were from diverse circles of interests. Some knew me from PTA and 4-H, some from my radio show, some from my days in community theater, others from my counseling practice and my in-home care agency, and still others from the women's gym. It seemed that everywhere I went there was a familiar face, someone who knew my history, someone who connected the dots of my life.

You know how it is when you get divorced—many of your couple's friends go away. That's pretty typical. Of course losing my best friend and her family created a void that I have yet to completely fill. But that's not the interesting part.

I have come to an understanding of myself that wasn't easy to admit. As the oldest child in a chaotic home, I learned early that the best way to stay safe was to adopt an attitude of strength and take on the responsibility of making sure everyone was happy and had what they needed. I know this is not news, people! As children, we make erroneous decisions about what we need to do and who we need to be in order to make sense of our experiences. It's impossible for a child to look at a dysfunctional parent and recognize the parent isn't ok. That parent is a God. He or she needs to be ok because our very survival depends on them being able to take care of us. So when there is a sense that something is wrong, we make it about ourselves rather than them.

My little girl said it's because of me that daddy is so angry. I need to listen better, eat faster, dress differently... etc. It's because of me that mommy is so sad. I need to be funnier, dance for her, brush her hair...etc. This is where my little girl decided that it was up to her to make the world happy. Wow! That's where the crazy making begins because of course she isn't capable of doing this big thing she's taken on.

And here's what I also realized as I looked back on the last 25 years: many of the people I attracted in my life needed me. They needed my strength, my willingness to work hard on their behalf, my determination to help them no matter what and some even needed my money... the list goes on. And I thought I wasn't asking anything in return, right? Wrong!!!!

I was asking them to love me and be loyal to me. I was asking not to be hurt or abandoned—all the things my little girl had been trying to avoid by taking care of others. But they did hurt me and abandon me. And looking back, I now know they had to because I wasn't really doing them or myself any good. I was playing the hero to their victim, which over time shifted. No one really wants to be rescued all the time. Most people eventually get tired of not being empowered. And in order to become their own hero, I had to become the person who was stopping them from getting their power, the villain. Wow!

Once they saw me as their villain, the only thing they

could do was become their own hero. What that meant was that the only place I could go from there was to eventually become their victim…and I did!

As you look at your life, does any of this resonate? I have found that those of us who become victims of another's antics usually have a deeper story of taking on more than we should, of believing that our value is tied up in how well we abandon ourselves and make other people's needs more important.

As I'm writing this and letting myself really feel into it, I have come to a "knowing" that the players in my story of betrayal may not have had any choice but to rebel against my heroism. Perhaps the cruelty, disloyalty and abuse were also just their way of reclaiming their inner hero. Now please understand I'm not blaming myself for their behavior. I'm not excusing them from their hurtful actions. There certainly were other ways of handling things. My friend could have just said she no longer wanted to be friend. My husband could have divorced me any of the three times I had offered to leave. But that's not what happened, and in a way, I'm beginning to understand why.

I am willing to look at my part. OMG…this is hard, right? I want to be so tender with myself in this moment because my instinct is screaming, "STOP…Remember what they did!"

However, some higher part of me is whispering something else. She's saying, "Darling, as long as you aren't able to see your part, you risk attracting more of

142

the same." You can't change your story if you don't see the truth in the one you've been living. Even if my part is only five percent of what went wrong, it's still my part.

As I look back on those relationships where I was betrayed, I can also now see how I felt resentment toward these people on an unconscious level. I'd given them so much of myself—my resources and time—and I didn't always feel that they loved me, included me, or accepted me. These of course were all emotions that I couldn't give to myself either. So why should the world give me more than I know how to accept? Hmmm.

Is it possible that until I can see my part and forgive myself, I will always be in this place of doubting that I can ever have love again? I don't want that.

Is it possible that, at last, I am coming to the core of my transformation process? I can sense for the first time as I write this that I can truly accept myself, flaws and all. I really can forgive myself because I only wanted what everyone wants. That's the key ladies! We all want love. We all want to belong. We all want to be understood, to matter and be valued just the way we are, but we are so addicted to that information coming to us from outside of ourselves. We have been so programed to wait for the world to tell us when we are ok, when we are pretty, when we are smart, when we are enough.

I used to pride myself in being a woman who was very trusting, comparing myself to others who said they can't trust anyone. I'd pat myself on the back and say I believe everyone deserves to be trusted until they show me otherwise. I have to tell you, sisters— I was deluding myself.

It wasn't that I trusted others. It was that I didn't trust myself. I couldn't depend on my intuition, my instincts, my knowing. I didn't have the experiences of a child who grew up trusting her environment and her ability to get what she needed. So, I deferred to others. But deep inside, that made me mad! I mean really irritated. So much so that although I didn't trust what I was feeling, I did trust what I was thinking, and I was more than happy to defend that! I can debate with the best of them, even if I don't quite believe my own stance. I can still make you think I know more than I know, and that's not really something I'm proud of. I share this with you now to illustrate how honest I am willing to be with myself, how transparent I am willing to be with you. And how, though I can tell you this, I am ok with who I am.

Even more important, there is evidence of what I'm saying because today the people in my world are drama free. They are not needy. They are powerful, strong, and successful. We are equals in all ways, which means I am no longer out there rescuing people in order to get love. I have given up the co-dependent hero in place of a loving woman who believes others are capable of taking care of themselves just as well as I am capable of receiving love.

Want more evidence? I no longer think of him. I no longer hear the questions that swirled in my head for years. I no longer feel anything when I see his name on a street sign. Oh yes, they are out there!

I have started dating again, but it does feel different. Maybe I'm more cautious; maybe I'm a little protective. Maybe this is what "healthy" looks like! Who knew! I'm still experimenting—not with the men, but with myself. Who am I in their presence? What part of me do they acknowledge and what part do they ignore? When do they shut me down and when do I have permission to sing?

Good questions right? Wrong! It's not about them. It's all about me! I know I've said this before, but it bears repeating...over and over...and over...until we really get it!

For years I have said that the only way for us to truly know ourselves is through relationship, and I really believe that. How else will I know if I'm funny but to elicit laughter from a friend? How else will I know the depths of my compassion but through my ability to help someone in pain? How else will I know the level of my generosity but through my giving to another? How will I know where my shadows lurk, where my pain hides, where my internal lies were born, but through the reflection in my lover's eyes?

So you see, to really know thyself, you have to be willing to be seen. And I mean warts and all. Because until we are willing to accept, love, forgive, trust, and know ourselves as the fully human, ego-based, amazing creatures that we are, what we will see in the world—in the faces of others—is our own projections and mirrors.

Furthermore, these people, who will come to show

us these parts of ourselves, are really angels we have known before, who though they may cause us pain in this life, may be necessary for our own growth.

I know that sounds crazy to some people, but I am surer of this now than I've ever been. I told you I experimented. I didn't go looking for a guy to experiment on. It wasn't like that at all. I genuinely wanted to fall in love and be with my soul mate. There is still a very tiny part of me that wonders if I can't find love does that mean that I am not healed, that he was right to treat me so badly. Omg...see how the mind still hangs on?

And in this instant, the best I can do is say, "Stop," lovingly of course, because I know none of that is true. The measure of who I am as a person isn't tied to anyone. The thoughts I have are powerless unless I believe them and act on them. And I don't, and I won't. 'Ya with me on this, ladies?

INSIGHTS:

We are such powerful creatures, and most of the time, we don't even know it. It is true that our brains have over 80,000 thoughts a day. Imagine trying to count those. And most of those thoughts go unnoticed by our conscious mind, thank God. Occasionally, some get through because we either think we have evidence or some emotion was triggered from our past experience.

What I have learned to do and am teaching my clients

is to ask some simple questions when a thought intrudes on your reality. Am I sure this is real? Is there any other possible explanation? Does thinking or feeling this without verification make me feel better or worse...does it serve me or does it hurt me? What else could it be besides what I'm thinking? Until I can confirm, what can I do to help myself in this moment?

I know that when I really ask myself these questions about something I'm telling myself, I get such clarity and can more easily shift my thoughts to what is true because the intruding thought usually is not.

In cases where I believe the negative thought is valid, I ask myself, "What can I do to change this (whatever it is) so that I feel better about who I am and can act with integrity?" This stops me in my tracks. Thoughts have power. Thoughts over time become things. I know that with all my heart, and I want to create consciously...by design, rather than by default. Don't you?

WHEN THE MIND IS SET FREE

In our world today, there isn't much time for contemplation. However, those of us on the heroine's journey come to know that reflection is an essential part of the task we have been sent to do. And when the story isn't about the past, your mind is set free to discover new things. So that's what I've been doing. Recently, three "ahas" have surfaced.

The first is that God, the Universe, Source, whatever you want to call that which is bigger than all, vibrates at a frequency of pure light and love. The frequency never lowers—never changes—is always emanating the highest good. Awesome, right?

Yet, when most of us pray—I mean really pray—we are down on our knees in great pain. Whether because of an illness, a loss of a job, the loss of a marriage, or the sheer helplessness of not knowing what to do, we cry to the heavens or whomever we believe is listening.

"Please God, make this stop…or fix my marriage… or help me find a job…or…"

And when we are in this state, we are vibrating at

a lower frequency than when we are experiencing joy and appreciation. What I learned is that from this lower frequency—this place of lack, this place of fear—God cannot meet me. Or better said—I cannot meet God. It's like being in a room that is devoid of light when the power goes out.

You know there is a light switch somewhere, but you cannot find the wall in the darkness. You are afraid to move toward it for fear of bumping into something that will hurt you. You keep asking and waiting for the power to go on, but you feel stuck. That switch is there—available always—but it cannot find you. It cannot change its location to meet you in the darkness.

But a candle can help you get there. A candle can light the way enough to guide you to the source of the light. To me, the candles are your angels. They can raise or lower their own vibrations to meet you where you are. So when we pray to them, even from a lower vibration—from the darkness in the powerless room—they can be that small candle showing us the way to the light switch. They are the bridge from our lower vibration of fear to the highest vibration of God, where all our prayers, both conscious and unconscious, are answered…always, even when the outcome is different than what we imagined.

The second thing I recently understood fully was that my reality—my current moment—is a reflection of all my thoughts, prayers, unconscious desires, and my feelings. If I don't like what I see in my current reality, the only way to change that is to change my focus. In other words, most of us pay close attention to what we are experiencing in the moment, and in doing so, it expands. It gets bigger and better, even when it's awful!

Our minds, like computers, are programmed to take in information and then associate it with something we already know. Its job is to file that information for further use. That's a great thing. It's what makes our lives work. It allows us to learn something new, like opening a door: we begin from a place of focusing consciously on completing the task and move toward a point at which we do the task automatically.

Imagine if that wasn't so. Imagine if every day everything you did each day was brand new. What if you had to literally think of every step which now comes automatically, without conscious thought? Every single thing you did would require a conscious decision and feel like the first time. Something like turning a doorknob would sound like this in your head: doorknob..reach out with hand and touch it...round... what does it do?...turn it....hmmm...pull it...oh...door opens....wow!

For those who have had strokes or memory loss, this is what life looks and feels like. Everything from picking up a fork and putting food in our mouths to meeting an old friend for coffee and talking about last year's party has no reference. It's like the movie *50 First Dates*, where everything from the heroine's "day before" is erased and all experiences and knowledge is happening right now for the first time. Can you imagine how difficult life would be?

So having this magnificent brain of ours which categorizes, memorizes, associates, and correlates—all the while without our conscious awareness—is truly a blessing and a gift. This brain filters so much information that we are gathering in every moment without us having to think about it.

But here is the dilemma. The choice of our brain's work in gathering information to assimilate into our understanding from emotions and thoughts is based on where we focus our attention. And so, if I'm focusing on how hard something is, then the brain responds by giving me all the validation I need from my reality to know my thought is true. If I focus my awareness on how great things are working out, my brain will gather all the information to validate that truth. It's like searching the web for facts on a subject. Depending on which side of the argument you focus your attention, you will find the data to support your argument. Always!

What I've learned from this is that I am in control of nothing outside my inner world except where I focus my attention. And whatever I focus on intentionally will become bigger and greater in my external world as my brain gathers more information to match that focus. I've played with this concept and found that depending on what I'm focusing on that day, life is full of fun, excitement, opportunities and joy, or fear, anxiety, loss, and powerlessness. Which do you choose? I invite you to play with this even for a day. What have you got to lose?

And finally, the third thing that I recently understood

was that when I ask the Universe, God, Source, for guidance and for signs that I am making the right decisions for my highest good, I always get an answer. I love that: the feeling that a miracle in the form of a coincidence has occurred, that I am not alone on my journey, and that my ultimate desire is to feel led toward those choices which will offer opportunities for me to expand and become more of who I am.

A lot of the time, the signs I perceive from the Universe validate what I consciously desire, and the outcome mirrors exactly what I wanted: a new house, a new love...a kitty cat! But recently, I have also experienced that the signs were there—so bright, so obvious— and yet, they led me down a path that was not, in my mind, where I wanted to end up.

When that happened, I thought and felt two things. One was that I couldn't trust the signs. They were not from the highest of high, but rather from my ego. And boy did that hurt. And it ultimately led me to doubt myself. The other was that I must have done something very wrong along the way to have ended up in this miserable place.

Does any of that sound familiar to you? The proverbial "they" say that hindsight is 20/20. In other words, it is only from the future that we can look back and say, "Wow, I would have done it differently." But would you have? What if instead we said, "Wow, I wouldn't be here today had I not followed that course."

We are always learning, always exploring ourselves in relation to the world. We can't truly know who we are without the experiences we have, both good and bad. Life would be boring if it was all easy, all happy, all gentle and soft. We need the bitter to appreciate the sweet. We need the loss to appreciate the win. We need the pain of sorrow to know the exquisiteness of joy. Yes, we live in a world of duality. I honestly can't imagine a world without it.

INSIGHTS:

And so what I discovered was that the final outcome of a path in my life—and there are many—was not what determined whether or not I am connected to the divine, or whether God heard my prayers, or if the signs were right and I can trust myself. It was never about the outcome. It was always about the journey. Was the journey important for my expansion? Was the journey, even though painful and not what I wanted, what ultimately gave me insight into more of who I am and what I am capable of? Was the journey necessary for me to move on to the next step toward the wholeness of me?

From that perspective and in answering those questions, I realized that the signs were perfect, that my guidance was always there. I followed these perfect signs thinking they would take me one place and found that instead they led me to something that wasn't what I knew I wanted. And, that something, was exactly what I needed. I couldn't really judge the experience, those involved, or myself without ultimately negating who I had become as a result. That was big!!!

These three insights have been part of my conscious

knowledge for quite a while. But they didn't become part of my inner understanding, my every day focus, my visceral knowing, until I lived them.

WHAT I'VE GAINED WHILE BECOMING

O k, so it's been two years since I've last added to this book. I could just say life got away from me. Not true. I could say I didn't have much to share. Also not true. Life always holds a place for us to experience the good and the bad. That is the nature of the duality of life on this planet. There are many reasons I haven't written. But the most important thing for you to know right now is that though I didn't write, it was not because I was still in pain. It was not because I had shut myself off from the world. It was not because my life was dreary, boring, or unhappy.

This is important for you to know because I have met women over the years who have suffered like I have and who after ten years had still not reclaimed their power. They were still living in a place of fear. They had been too scared to even date a man, let alone have a relationship again. Their lives were about maintaining instead of creating, about sustaining instead of inventing. And ladies, I didn't want that for me, and I don't want that for you. I want you to spread your wings as I have. I want you to know that there is an end to this transformational journey toward your highest potential. And so, here is what I've been doing the last two years.

My career has been growing both in selling real estate and coaching realtors. This came to me so easily that I felt it was meant to be. I was open to something new, something different, and it worked out well until it didn't. What? Yes, you heard me.

At first, it all felt like I'd finally landed on the tree I would live on for a while. I was learning new things and really enjoying my clients. Up to this point, I was also still receiving money from the business I still owned with my ex. Life was good. But that's usually when the shit hits the fan!

Yup. He started playing games with me again: not paying me on time, giving pity-party excuses, using fear tactics to get me to do what he wanted. He wanted me out of that business, and in the end—you know what—I wanted out too. I sold out for a third of what I should have received. I tried to fight it. I talked to attorneys, accountants, and other professionals who could see through his antics and agreed with my analysis of value. I could have fought it, but it would have cost me so much more than just money. In the end, none of it mattered. I could feel that old familiar feeling creeping back into my life: the fear and anxiety, the helplessness and the anger. I had to decide. You might someday have to make a similar decision. So here goes.

I had to decide if my sanity and well-being were worth the fight it would take to get the money I was owed or whether taking less and finally ending this connection would bring me the peace and stability I'd wanted over the last few years. In the end, I chose the latter. It would mean that I wouldn't be able to do some of the things I'd hoped to do when I finally got the money, but it also meant that I loved myself enough to not let money be more important than my well-being.

I won't pretend it was easy. There were days when I felt so cheated by him and by life. Some days all I wanted to do was sit stewing in my own pity-party. I would alternate between being mad at him for what he'd done and being mad at myself for allowing it. Sometimes life just felt unfair—like he had it all, and maybe that was because on some level I didn't deserve more. I'm sure you know what I'm talking about here. It starts as such a subtle feeling—one you really don't want to put words to, one you won't share with anyone else because they won't really understand. And even as I write this, I know that the feeling will pass. There is no real truth to it; it's just an old-patterned thought of doubt. Yes, it was part of the conditioning: a left-over from days now gone by, where the devastation of betrayal caused me to lose my confidence, my motivation, my faith in myself.

But now, it's not *him* causing these feelings. It's me. It's me questioning what I deserve. It's me that continues the litany of assault on myself. And it's up to me to shut it down, not by clamping down on the feelings—but by slowly taking every thought and challenging it with the truth.

What I realized is that no matter what I thought should have happened, in the end, I was still better off than I would have been otherwise. My life is no longer a jumble of nerves waiting for the metaphorical shoe to drop. I'm no longer diligently scanning for clues about what someone needs in order to feel good so that I'm safe.

I look around at my adorable place, where every room has a purpose; everything in the room is something that has meaning to me. I feel the essence of the space I've created in my life where things are calm and tranquil, where I entertain new friends, where laughter and creativity, tenderness and honesty dwell. And I soften. My thoughts relax...my body calms and my breath comes easier. And I let go. Again...and again...and again.

I took the money, and I closed that door for the final time. I was no longer in any way connected to this man, except through my memories. And I was the one who got to decide which I would share, which I would enjoy remembering, and which I would let go of.

What was even more interesting was that once I so easily identified the old feelings in this exchange, I could now more easily see the same toxic antics of others in my life. Perhaps they were a little more subtle and not so up close and personal, but still there. I was starting to get a clear vision of my own personal boundaries. I was the manager of my own priorities, and I didn't have to fight for the things that were true for me about who I am and how I wanted to be treated. I just had to claim them, and when they weren't honored, I needed to bless the situation or person and move on.

And that led me to another breakthrough where I once again said no to something that meant I was saying yes to me, even though it cost me financially because in the end money is never a good enough reason for being less than I can be. So I left my job and went out on my own, and that has been a blessing. My practice has grown through referrals, and I truly love what I do.

Each time I saw situations, people, organizations, and even men, who were not in alignment with my values, I was able to acknowledge the differences and step away. The need to fight for my existence—to justify my being here, to prove my value, to receive love—just slowly disappeared.

INSIGHTS:

In the world we live in today, not knowing what enough means to us leaves us vulnerable to the opinions, offerings, persuasions, and goals of others. This is one of those big issues that most people don't want to talk about. I think because they think it's about limitation, but I don't see it that way. I see it more like one might look at boundaries.

When I sit down at a meal, if I don't know when I'm full, I will be forever enticed to have that extra piece of cake, that third glass of wine, etc. And that may not seem to be a problem until it translates to 30 pounds I have a hard time getting rid of.

The same is true with anything in excess. Our bodies tell us, if we listen, when we've exercised "too" much. Our bank account or credit limit tells us when we've spent too much. Our family tells us when we are working too much because they never see us. When we don't know what is "enough" for ourselves, we can't possibly know when someone else's behavior is "too much" for us to handle—when we're saying yes too much to someone else's agenda, when we can't say no because we don't know if now is the time to say no.

We each have to decide. How much money do you need to be comfortable and happy? How much food do you need to be satiated? How much exercise do you need to stay healthy? How much attention do you need to feel loved?

Conversely, how many lies are enough to make you be honest with yourself? How much giving can you do before you are all tapped out? How many times will you allow someone to put you down before you have the confidence to say stop?

Enough goes both ways. Boundaries are just a way to enforce something. Your values, your beliefs, and your criteria are the things we measure "enough" from. And the measures of "enough" and "too much" are what we are enforcing! So begin asking what is enough for me and what is too much for me?

So many times I've heard people talk about boundaries as if they are a physical circle made of bricks that we have erected around us. These boundaries are how we keep people from hurting us. Many times people feel that because they were unable to say no and got hurt, the problem was deficient boundaries. So they set up very strong ones to keep themselves safe. But here's what I've found. When the boundaries are rules that we have placed between us and the world, they can keep us isolated—separate—and because that goes against what our soul desires, at some point, we will tear that wall down. It will feel too confining, too foreign to us, too limiting to define us.

When we are clear about what enough is—what our inner values, criteria, needs and wants are—we will no longer sacrifice ourselves. We no longer need to clarify, re-commit, or justify. There is no actual boundary...no wall. We just are being our authentic selves, and we know what is true for us. We don't have to push people away or hold them back in order to continue to protect ourselves from the pain of abandoning who we are. Our knowing of ourselves is so strong that it needs no defense. Imagine how amazing that feeling must be. This is also a practice I invite you to bring into your life. The question is always...what do I want? So simple...yes?

THINGS THAT COME TO ME AS I FLY...

I'm sitting on the back porch of a hundred year old farmhouse looking out across what once was an avocado orchard, just thinking about my life. As I sit here, a soft summer breeze is wrestling the trees, and the dogs are sunbathing. I'm here at my 85 year old mom's house. My mom fell and broke a hip, and since my work is mobile, I came down to help her. She's doing great and doesn't really need me but because I lived so far away and haven't spent a lot of time with her over the past 30 years, I thought this would be a great time to create memories with her.

I have grown and healed in so many ways through this transformational journey. I feel no resentment, no bitterness, no fear. My work is fulfilling, and my kids are doing great; I really feel content with my life. I love my alone time and have always been able to fill it with projects, writing, and creating. I have a handful of amazing friends who are great fun, wonderful support and able to hold me accountable.

I am still waiting for the love of my life. I've had several men come in—each an opportunity to learn in some way or another. Some taught me big things and stayed for a while. Others were just pit stops, dropping reminders of who I've become. I'm not saying that this is the best way to heal, but as I said earlier in this book, relationships are the fastest way for you to experience yourself.

Each of these men was a gift to me, and I will forever be grateful for what I learned.

One was funny and masculine and still striving to prove himself. I was very attracted to him because he was smart and strong and a little defiant. But I quickly saw that he really wasn't ready for a relationship, and I would have been in an uphill battle to prove I was worthy of his love. Phew...an old pattern released...I finally got it and knew I didn't need to prove anything to anyone. But we remained friends, and that's nice.

The next one actually put a ring on my finger. He was very intelligent, very fatherly, and understood my work because he was a coach too. He adored me, but over time, I could see how insecure he was, how much of my attention he needed—how much control he needed, and I knew it wasn't going to work. The amazing thing was I didn't have to defend, try to change, make excuses... none of it. I just went along being me, and eventually, he realized we weren't going to work. I'm sad to say he was pretty hurt, but even that I didn't take on as my own.

The next one was a funny guy. He was the guy who made you laugh, was always looking for the next fun thing to do, treated all women with respect, and wanted to be everyone's hero. I'm an introvert and don't need a lot of excitement around me, so his whirlwind adventurous nature was fun...but tiring. And the gift from this man was that I became clear about one of the things I wanted in a relationship. I want to matter. My partner will always be the most important person in my life, and I want to be the same priority to him. This was something he could not give me. We parted as friends too, though we lost contact.

And then there was the man who rescued me. I was sick with walking pneumonia that went undiagnosed for four months when we met. I was weak, in pain, and really in need of someone to take care of me, and he did it so beautifully. He loved being needed, and I did need him. Once I got well though, things didn't go as smoothly. There were so many differences between us. I had grown to love who I am enough not to negate my own desires for his. That doesn't mean I wasn't willing to adapt and take turns, but being so different, the dynamic was difficult at best. And then I fell and broke my collarbone. Once again, things got better between us, and that's when I saw the future in this relationship. I'd have to be sick or broken so that he could take care of me, and I wasn't willing to make a life on that. Through this relationship, I saw that as much as I wanted to "matter," I also didn't want to have to give my power away in exchange for it. I have to be loved for my strength as well as my weaknesses. So, we parted as friends too.

At this point, I really was starting to feel that perhaps

I wasn't capable of falling in love. My mind would race with memories of each encounter and ask...am I shut down emotionally...am I forever so scarred that I can't love again...are my criteria too much...my standards too high?

And that's when the next one appeared. Now this one was different. I'd known him as a friend for ten years. We both lived in the same town I'd moved from, and both moved away within a few years of each other. We'd kept in touch through Facebook over the years. So when I was making a trip to Denver on business and found out he lived there, we reconnected.

There are a lot of details from which I will spare you, but what is important to know is that this man was again a very important gift and part of my final piece of healing. Because I already knew him and we shared common friends, trust didn't really have to be built. It was almost automatic. I had always enjoyed his company as a friend and because we were both in relationships when we met that was all there ever was between us back then. We share a spiritual path, a common philosophical view of life, and some pretty cool dreams. The romance was fast, deep, and sexual. This was the first man since my divorce that I could honestly say I was fully physically attracted to. And in a short period of time, I had fallen in love. So you see... the answers to the questions I'd had were answered. I was capable of love. It just had to be the right person.

So what happened right? Well...as fast as that candle was lit, it blew out at the first sign of darkness. I saw certain behaviors and incongruence that were very familiar to me. They were there with my ex, and they were there with the mountain man. I never saw them with my ex because I was far too invested. I saw them with the mountain man because I was more invested in me. And though it really broke my heart again, I saw it with this dear old friend too. I did give it a try. I am so clear that while it takes two to make a relationship, it only takes one to break it. And so it was over before it barely began, but I learned so much about what I am capable of creating.

Many would look at my track record over the last few years and perhaps wonder about my sanity, my capacities, my values, etc. And that's ok. I'm way past caring what others think. But a dear, dear friend and a father figure to me said recently, "You amaze me, Ali. No matter how many times you are disappointed, you never give up on love. You have one of the biggest hearts I've ever known." And you know what, he's right...I won't give up!

INSIGHTS:

I felt this piece was so important to share. I wonder if you've ever lost a job you loved. Or maybe you wanted to get on a team, or tried out for a play and didn't get either. Did that make you stop? Did you give up on all future jobs? Did you stop playing team sports? Did you never try out for another part? I'm betting the answer is no. You were hurt. You were disappointed. You may have even taken a punch to your confidence, but that didn't stop you. So why let one man...one betrayal...or two...or four not-your-prince-men stop your search for the love of your life?

At the beginning of my dating experiences, when I saw or felt something I didn't want, as I've already told you, I got out. But not just out. I got out quickly. I didn't realize the significance of the "quick get-away" until now. You see, for those of us who stayed too long, who ignored the signposts, who lowered our bar...and then were betrayed, learning to leave without beating ourselves up or letting someone else flatten us before we go—that's a big thing!!!

When we were children, we couldn't leave. We didn't have the resources, the knowledge, the power to say, "I'm out of here...you are not ok." But as grown-ups, we do. We don't have to stay in a job that kills our spirit and tears down our bodies. We don't have to stay in a relationship that steals our power and breaks our hearts. But we do have to be willing to be uncomfortable, out of control, maybe a little scared, unsure, and willing to make a mistake when we are learning how to be true to ourselves, to be our own champion, to ask for what we want, and to listen to that little voice inside. So at the beginning, that may mean you've got to move quickly. You've got to say it's ok to leave. It doesn't matter how many relationships, how many jobs, how many times you have to say "no" before getting to "your big yes." As you practice, you will begin to feel safer and more in control; you will feel empowered to act on your choices and able to respond appropriately over time.

Now of course, you get to decide. If you really don't want another relationship, then that's fine. I'm not one who believes *you are not complete until you have a man. In fact, recently I told myself that I had a year to find my true love because I really feel I'm ready but that if he didn't show up before my next birthday…well…then I was going to be just fine, and my back-up plan would go into effect. Why? Because I believe that a wish is a prayer, and a prayer is answered as long as we take action. I am fine with either outcome, but the actions may be different. So that's my plan. But you make yours…only you know what your heart truly wants.*

The Next Butterfly Quest

Nothing has changed, and everything has changed. As I sit here today and write, I realize that I am no longer the woman I used to be. I still have the same talents and gifts, my knowledge and experiences still part of my repertoire, but how I see the world, how I respond to others, how I am with myself...all different.

Try as I might to feel the feelings of devastation I did almost six years ago on that fateful day, I cannot. I can remember it all as if it was yesterday, but I cannot feel it in my body. I no longer feel my heart racing, my breath cut short, my hands shaking. Instead I feel peace, a gentleness with myself that I've never known before. Sometimes I ask myself, "Have I just suppressed it all?"

And the answer is a resounding NO. I have just transformed it.

Like the caterpillar who no longer exists after its metamorphosis, I too no longer exist the way I used to. I have found my voice, my true North, my strength. I have loved my vulnerability, my shadows, my inner child. And just as I have changed, my worldview has shifted from the smallness of a leaf to the openness of the skies. Still, it feels odd, peculiar sometimes. I can get glimpses of the old me, and sometimes she even acts up if I haven't given her enough attention. But she is endearing, and I'm delighted rather than ashamed or repulsed by her unabashed queries. She does help me stay accountable at times too. And you know what? It's ok not to know it all sometimes. It's ok to occasionally throw yourself a little pity-party for old time's sake. But you won't stay there, not if you've done the work.

We must be willing to see and feel the bigger picture of our relationships within our journey. As I say that, I know that I am ready to open my heart once more, to take a chance, to try out my new wings.

As I wrote in the last chapter, I've been having some serious discussions of late with God about my love life. I struck a deal with him. Now before you go saying that's not possible, let me just say, it is! I made a deal with God thirty-five years ago when I asked for a daughter after giving birth to three beautiful little boys.

I said, "God, if having a daughter is part of my destiny, then let me get pregnant before the end of this year. If I don't, I'll know that any future child will be another boy!"

Before the year was over, I was pregnant with my sweet little girl. Unlike everyone else I had shared this information with at the time, I never had a doubt that my prayers would be answered.

My most recent deal with God to help me attract a "forever" guy stems from the realization that every man

I've met since my divorce offered me an opportunity to grow. I can see that in the process of becoming a "better me," my "guy" is becoming better too!

Now I'm not saying this one is "the one," but the guy I met four months ago is pretty special. We met online, but currently, we are living in some pretty weird times. Social distancing and masks are the orders of the day due to the pandemic called Covid19, and since I live with an 86 year old, precautions are important.

So, our first date was like no other. Instead of meeting at a Starbucks for coffee or a restaurant for a glass of wine, we met on zoom and had a six hour conversation over a virtual glass of wine. I think we were both feeling a little like teenagers, but nothing about our budding relationship is childish. He is someone with whom I can envision a beautiful life. To be honest, it feels great. So many parts of me have come alive with him. He's awakened the sensual/sexual woman I am, which has also stirred my creativity and strengthened my power. And I'm loving all of it. After all my experiences these last years meeting men and getting clear about what I want in a relationship, the thing I noticed about this man, is how he seems to embody the best quality of each of the men I've dated. In a funny way it's like my "man order" is complete. In so many ways, we are equally yoked. Our past stories are similar, and our values are in alignment. We laugh easily with each other, support each other's work life, and find ease in the quiet between us. And what is most interesting and exciting is that we both have held the same dream of the life we want to create, filled with retreats and alpacas!

What's really amazing to me is how much I feel connected to him and completely aware of myself at the same time. How effortlessly I can tell him how I feel and ask for what I want. I do not bend into a pretzel to make him love me, and I do not need his words of love to feel secure. I am not abandoning myself to meet his needs, and I'm not containing my feelings to protect myself from being hurt. I live in the now, and the now is …not good… not bad…but always perfect!

So even though I don't know where this relationship will go, what I can say is that as much as it is filling me up, exciting me, and enticing me to dream again…I also know that if it ended tomorrow, I would be ok. Between you and me, I hope he is the one, but I hold no attachments and have no expectations. I'm just enjoying the experience and looking forward to each new part of the adventure.

Meanwhile, I have come back to my home town to finish this book. When I left years ago a broken woman, devastated and not knowing where my life was leading me, I wasn't sure if I could ever come back here. I couldn't imagine a day when the memories of what was, would no longer haunt me.

But today as I sit here looking out the my window at mountain peaks and tall pines, hearing birds singing and feeling the warmth of the sun, my heart feels warm too. It has been such a long journey. From this perfect little cottage, I can readily see the blessings of my life. And they are not at all the things I believed were important to me. That's the surprising thing about life.

I started this journey of transformation fighting and kicking, telling the world this was not what I wanted—it was not what was supposed to be. I have to laugh. Oh, what a naïve, silly girl I was. Back then, I believed my life would look like this: A happy long term marriage... not...a beautiful family home...not...money in a 401k for my retirement...not...grown kids, married with children...not. I was going to be the quintessential retired professional—traveling, entertaining, spending time with the grandkids...not!

A part of me believed that until I had those things again I was not a success—I was not healed...I was not ready to serve others.

This life I imagined was supposed to be the reward for all my hard work, the pinnacle of my success. It was the life we were programmed to strive for. When all of that went away, I had lost my identity, my direction, my reason for getting out of bed in the morning. And the craziest part of all of this was that even though I was completely miserable in that old life, I convinced myself I wasn't. You understand that, right?

And down the long and winding road to me...to now...I see my identity is not connected to anyone...not a man, not my kids, not my work, not my money or my home. That the criteria I use to measure my journey are very different than what they used to be.

This has been a journey of self-love, forgiveness, and

trust, of rediscovering my authentic self, of redefining my connection with myself and others, and of reinventing my life through honoring my power. This is what it means to heal, to thrive, to begin again, anew. I have arrived. I'm not done...far from it. But I really do like me! I have no illusions or expectations. I am so grateful you've been here with me. I hope with all my heart that along the way I have given you something worth your time. You have so much to give, and this is your time to step into your brilliance. Sometimes we do have to be broken open to let the diamond shine.

Taking in the aroma of the fresh Oregon air, listening to the flapping wings of the hummingbirds as they flutter in place at the honey feeders, I feel so at peace. I have no need to confront any old stories or restrict any painful memories. The past is finally where it belongs...in the past. And my senses are filled with the beauty of the present moment. I can feel my joy forming a smile on my face and tears in my eyes. My perfect peace is only interrupted by one thing...a butterfly. She lands by my feet in a potted plant and slowly moves her wings back and forth as if saying...

"Welcome home. You have done it!"

It's been one hell of a Butterfly Quest!

FINAL INSIGHTS:

Since finishing this book, I have broadened the scope of my work to include coaching women who have come through betrayal and are still stuck in the strategy stage. They have found a sense of stability, let go of some of the anger, and accepted some of what happened...

However, they have yet to accept the new normal that is their lives: have yet to rediscover their full potential; have yet to build the self-love and self-trust that brings them to self-forgiveness; have yet to find happiness, love, and purpose. And I do believe with all my heart—from what I've seen in others and what I've experienced in myself—that the journey is worth it. The world needs us to be who we came here to be before we were programmed and conditioned to play small. So this is your time. The world is waiting for you.

So what does it really mean to be born of betrayal? Ultimately, it is to give birth—through the breakdown caused by betrayal—in order to breakthrough to the you that is meant to live the authentic, connected, and empowered life you came here to live. This is the heroine's journey, and one that many of us have to go through because we have much to share with the world.

This metamorphosis begins with a devastating event that shifts our worldview enough to launch us into crucial self-examination, which leads us to self-acceptance and is key to experiencing inner freedom.

We have to look at how we set up negative patterns in our lives due to a deep inner trauma that is usually connected to our childhood when we felt unsafe and unacceptable in some way. These conditioned responses were survival strategies that we adapted to try to earn the love we so deserved.

We have to go through the exploration of the event to get to the place in which we can honestly see that what happened isn't really about "them or him," but instead about us. This is where we find the cosmic wound that we have come here to heal and that perhaps "they/he" was sent to help us heal it. This applies whether the cause of the betrayal was a spouse, partner, boss, employee, or even your body. This is important to understand because— while they are responsible for their behaviors—unless we address the crux of our pain and fear, we will continue to find ourselves in similar patterns with other relationships.

Remember that whatever time it takes to go through this transformation is the time it takes. There is no rule of thumb, no average, no right amount of time to experience this growth. There is no time limit or linear process. So we have to stop beating ourselves up for how long it takes to get to the point where we no longer define ourselves by this event. Just allow yourself to feel and be kind to yourself through all of it.

That's when the magic happens…when we accept where we landed. We are able to forgive ourselves, find the gems in the experience, and finally forgive others too. We know forgiveness has happened because we no longer have a visceral feeling in our body. Remember our body cannot lie. It will let us know if we still feel unsafe (forgiveness hasn't happened) or feel completely safe (forgiveness has occurred). It's really that simple.

It's important to know that the memory of your experience

will not go away. And just as you smile and maybe even laugh when you tell an old story that made you happy, you may still get sad or angry when you tell this story from time to time. But the key here is that you don't get stuck in that story. It no longer takes up real estate in your head. It doesn't stop you from creating something new for yourself...a job, a relationship, a home, a friendship. You are now becoming someone new...and it's ok to be tentative about this new life.

Within us, even as caterpillars, the tiniest of wings exist, symbolizing our highest selves just waiting for us to agree to enter the goo—the void, the painful part of this journey. And though it may feel at times that we are alone, God/Spirit/Universe has sent us EVERYTHING we need to navigate this pain.

This is work that cannot be done for you, ladies. There is no magic bullet, no easy button. This thing called transformation is messy. It's hard work. It's a time of finding meaning in the things that have happened to us...both good and bad. It's a time of recognizing what we want and what we fear—a time to accept our shadows and weaknesses. It's about taking responsibility for our actions and inactions, for the mistakes we made and the pain we allowed. All of this is what must happen in order for us to get through the process of letting go of the caterpillar life that no longer serves us, step into the cocoon—where from the void the transformation happens—and emerge to become the magnificent and powerful women we are, living the highest expression of ourselves. This is what the world is waiting for. We are the future...we have the power to change worlds. We can be the difference. Come on, ladies...let's fly!

The butterfly at the end of her journey
finds the tree from which her caterpillar self
came…and there she lays her eggs…
Starting the process of transformation all
over again.
Only knowing through her divine instinct
that this is what she's here to do.
And letting it be so…
Without fear…without force…without
expectation…
Just a new life…emerging once more…

ACKNOWLEDGEMENTS:

This is the place in which gratitude is spoken, and yet most people rarely read this very important part of the book. I hope this sentence will serve as an interesting enough opening to invite you to continue. Because here is the thing—while we go through the devastation of betrayal, the crashing down of the life we knew, the upside down of our worldview—I know we feel alone. We feel at times that no one is there, and no one understands; no one can help us. But the truth is we were never alone. And I hope this serves as a reminder for you to look around and give thanks for those who are silently praying, gently holding your hand, and tenderly stepping in to help you out when you most need it.

I first give thanks to God, my guides, my angels, my ancestors...those of other worlds who stood by and touched me with healing, whispered inspiration, unlocked my dreams, and showed me the way through the darkness of my soul.

I thank my dear mother, my children, my siblings,

their spouses and my cousin for coming to my side the instant my world fell apart, for holding me up when I couldn't stand, for helping me financially when I had no support, and for always believing in my strength and goodness even when I forgot it was there.

I thank my dearest friends—you know who you are—for your loyalty and trust, for your desire to make me laugh through the tears, propel me forward into my dreams, and making sure I knew you would catch me if I fell.

I thank my coaches, counselors, and mentors for holding the mirror while I saw myself for the last time and the first time and loving me through my journey.

I thank all the people who helped me write this book: the people who read the manuscript and told me to publish, those who helped make my words clear, my amazing editor and publisher, those who shared their betrayal experience with me, and those who allowed my story to guide their way to their own transformation.

And finally I want to say a special thanks to my dear friend Urmi whose art adorns the front cover of this book. Her beautiful painting, hanging on her wall, was ultimately the inspiration for the title of this book.

ABOUT THE AUTHOR

Ali Davidson is a best-selling author, transformational coach, international speaker, and a dynamic presenter. She knows that transformation is an inside job that each of us goes through at some point in our lives. An endlessly inquisitive student, intuitive seeker and a believer that life is meant to be fun, Ali draws on many years of personal coaching, her own experience and intuitive wisdom to develop a philosophy that inspires, motivates and heals the heart.

As a child of an alcoholic and a survivor of incest, Ali has known tremendous pain and the disruption of the life she imagined through divorce, bankruptcy, the loss of the company she co-founded and the home she raised her children in. Like so many, she knows firsthand what it feels like to lose it all, be plunged into the chaos of the cocoon, and emerge as the butterfly she was meant to be. By triumphing over her own trauma, Ali has found what works and now teaches others how to spread their wings.

Her training and certifications include: Master Practitioner of Neuro-Linguistics Programming, certified personal coach, trained in the Art of Feminine Presence, Mars/Venus relationship coach and a certified hypno-therapist. She has been coaching and counseling for over 25 years.

Ali loves working with women individually and in groups. Her greatest love is in-depth retreats where together Ali and her participants can learn, transform, and expand into their highest potential.

If you would like to communicate with Ali you may email her at ali@coachalidavidson.com. You may also set a Complimentary exploration session by visiting https://calendly.com/bornofbetrayal/30-minute-exploration-session to set an appointment.